The INDIAN HUNTERS

Dedication

To my parents for initiating my interest in our Native Americans and the great out-of-doors, and to my wife for sharing the wilderness experience with me and being an inspiration in the writing of this book.

R. Stephen Irwin, M.D.

A lifelong pursuit of sport fishing and big game hunting coupled with an intense interest in the Indians and Eskimos of North America made the subject matter of *The Providers* a natural topic for Dr. Irwin.

Dr. Irwin has a B.A. degree in zoology from Indiana University and is a graduate of Indiana University Medical School. He practised family medicine in his hometown of Roachdale, Indiana, for eleven years.

A prolific freelance writer of outdoor material, Dr. Irwin has been published in *Guns, Fur-Fish-Game, Safari, Sports Afield,* and other sporting journals.

In addition to hunting, fishing and collecting Indian artifacts and sporting memorabilia, Dr. Irwin enjoys racing stock cars on dirt tracks. Dr. Irwin's wife Jan is an avid outdoorswoman and accompanies him on his extensive travels throughout North America. Currently they reside on Flathead Lake near Polson, Montana.

J.B. Clemens

J.B. Clemens has spent a lifetime portraying Native Americans and the wilderness. The authenticity of his works appeals to naturalist, historian and art lover alike. He has completed commissions for the Abraham Lincoln Foundation and Bi-Centennial Commission, and has painted large historical murals for the Milwaukee Public Museum, Oshkosh Public Museum, Indiana State Museum and the Children's Museum of Indianapolis. Currently, J.B. is painting commissions for discriminating collectors of western and wildlife art. His oils hang in many important collections.

The INDIAN HUNTERS

Hunting and Fishing Methods of the North American Natives

R. Stephen Irwin, M.D.

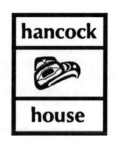

hancock

house

ISBN 0-88839181-1 Paperback
ISBN 0-88839-183-8 Hardcover
Copyright © 1984 R. Stephen Irwin

Second printing 1994

Cataloging in Publication Data
Irwin, R. Stephen
    The Indian hunters
    Hunting and fishing methods of the North
    American natives

    Includes index.
    Bibliography: p.
    ISBN 0-88839-181-1 Paperback
    ISBN 0-88839-183-8 Hardcover

    1. Indians of North America—Hunting. 2. Indians
of North America—Fishing. 3. Indians of North
America—Trapping. 4. Inuit—Hunting.* 5. Inuit
—Fishing.* 6. Inuit—Trapping.* I. Clemens, J. B.
II. Title.
E98.H8178   639'.1'08997   C83-091134-0
                                  C83-091149-9

Cover art: Susanne Lansonius

Published simultaneously in Canada and the United States by

HANCOCK HOUSE PUBLISHERS LTD.
19313 Zero Avenue, Surrey, B.C. V4P 1M7
(604) 538-1114   Fax (604) 538-2262

HANCOCK HOUSE PUBLISHERS
1431 Harrison Avenue, Box 959, Blaine, WA 98231-0959
(206) 354-6953   Fax (604) 538-2262

Contents

Acknowledgements

As in an army where many show courage but only a handful are decorated, so in this book only a few can be formally acknowledged although many have contributed generously.

Kathy Bean of Depauw University was immensely valuable in assisting me with library research. Mary Code was instrumental in the translation of several Athapaskan terms. Dr. Susan Sutton of the IUPUI Anthropology Dept. furnished a most helpful technical critique. Leo Johnson of the Milwaukee Public Museum and Bob Hruska and Kitty Hobson of the OshKosh Public Museum aided in researching the ethnographic photo files of their fine museums. Mrs. Dixie Green assisted in locating some excellent historical photos. Mr. Don Wilson, horticulturist, offered information on many plants used by the Native Americans. Dr. James Mason made helpful editorial suggestions and Saundra Hoopengarner and Paula Hartman helped with clerical duties.

Special thanks are due the many explorers, adventurers, naturalists, ethnologists and Native Americans who have been keen in their observations, thorough in their recording, and who have often endured considerable hardship in the course of their studies.

An Eskimo from Nunivak Island prepares to hurl his spear while open-water sealing from a kayak. Denver Public Library — Western History Department Photo by Edward Curtis

Introduction

Our technical society is flourishing, there is no doubt about that. The earliest ancestors of man struggled through the Stone Age and into the Metal Age. Advances during that era led to the Agricultural Revolution and this in turn to the Industrial Revolution. Currently, we are living in the scientific or technical era and our capabilities and pool of knowledge grows at an exponential rate. The greatest question now facing mankind is: can we survive our successes? Will we continue to live harmoniously or will we deplete our sustaining resources? Will our wastes and byproducts poison our environment to a point that is incompatible with life? Or — most horrible of all horrors —will we exterminate ourselves with a sudden nuclear holocaust? The certainty of our survival or our demise is not known, and perhaps that is a blessing. Still, extinction of the human race remains a haunting possibility.

It is not unreasonable that at some future time, perhaps millennia from now, cosmic archaeologists will visit our devastated planet and start sifting through jumbled piles of concrete and steel. These scientists will mark the straight paths of debris-covered asphalt that were our highways and puzzle over the silted-in lake beds behind huge crumbled dams. Perhaps they will be amused at the varying styles of automobile bodies they excavate and intrigued by our burial customs. If they are thorough in their diggings and their information correct, if their deductions are accurate about the life that was once on earth, even we might be startled at their conclusions.

The story of man's time on earth pieced together from our stratum of remains would show that cultural man lived for 2,000,000 years. All but the last 10,000 years, or 99% of

Hunters of the World

10,000 B.C.

World Population: 10 million
Per Cent Hunters: 100

1500 A.D.

World Population: 350 million
Per Cent Hunters: 1.0

his entire time on earth, he lived successfully by gathering and by hunting other animals. Only in those most recent 10,000 years did he learn agricultural practices, the domestication of animals and the use of metal tools. Concomitantly with these developments, there was a decline in the long-standing, stable, hunting life and a subsequent flowering of technology that, on the full time scale of man on earth, would coincide almost identically with his demise.

Until 10,000 years ago, essentially every earthling survived by hunting. By the time of Christ, 8,000 years later, only half of the human race was dependent on hunting and this number continued to dwindle until the last 300-400 years when only isolated pockets of hunting cultures existed around the world. There was a worldwide trend towards an increasing dependency on horticulture, particularly in the more temperate climates. In spite of this, of the approximately 80,000,000,000 humans who have ever lived on earth to date, 90% survived by hunting. (The word hunting here is used in the broadest sense to include fishing and trapping.) It seems inconsistent that such little is

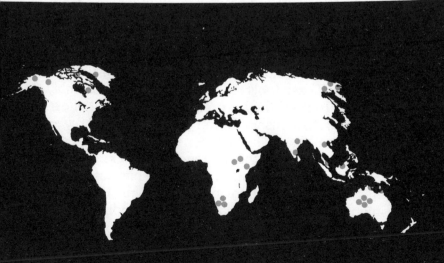

1900   World Population: 3 billion
Per Cent Hunters: 0.001

known about the technology of the economy that has been vital to the bulk of humanity. There is a lack of information on hunting, fishing and trapping techniques among hunting cultures of the last two centuries that were available for study. While the literature is replete with descriptive accounts of primitive art, social structure, mythology, linguistics, etc., apparently many early ethnographers found daily working routines essential for survival too mundane to record.

It has been customary to view hunting cultures as primitive, even inferior, particularly if they have crumbled under the weight of a more complex society. Still, that a hunting life has produced the longest running and, to date, most stable means of subsistence cannot be denied. What could be a greater achievement? Primitiveness, like beauty, is in the eye of the beholder.

As a predator, man was poorly equipped by nature. Most of his prey were both faster and stronger than he. For success, man the hunter had to develop highly complex physical and mental skills. Only through years and generations of evolutionary development did expertise in searching, stalking, retrieving, butchering and preparing for use acquire their ultimate sophistication. These skills were coupled with a knowledge of animal anatomy and behavior, as well as weather forecasting. Finally, this entire repertoire had to be passed on to man's offspring through proper childhood training.

The task of hunting required a relatively advanced weaponry. These tools for survival were no assembly line products. Rather, they represented individual effort and personal craftsmanship. Better ideas with more rewarding results were gleaned from experience, and these improvements were a part of the heritage of the next generation.

It was the brain of man that made him superior to his prey. He had the ability to observe, to think, to plan, and to fashion at first crude, then advanced, weapons. He learned how to be a more effective hunter by cooperating in groups. Such skills separated man from other predators in the animal kingdom and were the embryo for all future technologies.

The Providers is an attempt to record and to illustrate the hunting, fishing and trapping methods of the Indians and Eskimos of North America. While a geographic division has provided the best organization, it does result in an imbalance due, in part, to the varying importance of hunting as opposed to horticulture in a given region.

The Pueblos in the Southwest, for example, depend almost entirely on farming for their subsistence. An occasional rabbit drive offered about the only exception. A diversity of terrain and the presence of a variety of game animals fostered many different kinds of techniques in other areas. Also, the amount of early recorded data for research differs among geographic locations. Specifically, in the Eastern United States, acculturation was so rapid and so complete that much of the way those Indians lived has been lost forever.

Culture is never static, but is constantly undergoing change, sometimes slowly, and at other times very rapidly. At any given moment many factors are interacting with a given culture to give it individuality. The descriptions in this text of the traditional hunting and fishing lifestyles of Indians (and Eskimos) in the pre-contact era can only be an educated reconstruction of their actual methods. As time passes, facts become more obscure, memories dim and any such reconstruction of life before the influence of traders and explorers becomes subject to greater conjecture. Only a veiled image is presented by historical documents, artifacts and ethnographic studies. Of necessity, when dealing with large geographic areas containing numerous tribes or groups, many generalizations must be made about native Americans. It would take volumes to adequately describe the life of even a single

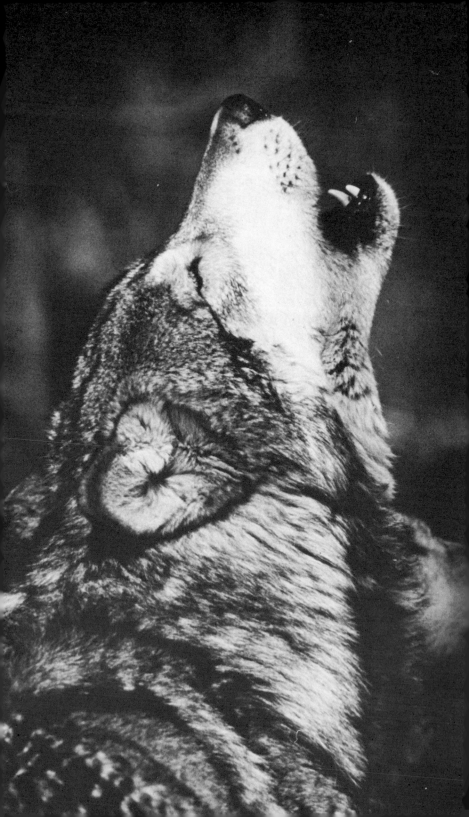

group of these people. Many regional variations and specializations must therefore be ignored in this work. Furthermore, it can not be assumed that the descriptions of tools, methods, or lifestyles applies to all the groups within a geographic area.

If some of the methods described in this book seem cruel or barbaric, we must remind ourselves that our own society is no less savage. Advanced technology may allow us to be more discreet in our slaughter, and it may be performed by proxy using select executioners, but our requirements for survival are no different from those of the native Americans. We, like they, must continue to provide.

Elk Tom Hall

Appearance of Man in North America

North America was once a continent that had never known man. Then at some unrecorded moment, at a time that is almost unimaginably long ago, the New World first felt the tread of a human foot. These intrepid wanderers became the first Americans. They were primitive big game hunters from Siberia, gaining access to the North American Continent by the way of Bering Strait, between 25,000 and 40,000 years ago.

It was in the Old World, specifically in Africa, where man evolved. Much later, he migrated into the New World. That Bering Strait is the most likely location for this migration has been substantiated by considerable archaeological evidence, and the feasibility of such a feat is apparent if one consults a map of the area. Only 56 miles (90 kilometers) of water separate the continents of Asia and North America at Bering Strait; even this expanse of water is broken up in the middle by the Diomede Islands.

Today, such a distance would not make a very impressive boat trip, but it is doubtful that these primitive hunters had a craft capable of even this meager voyage. During the Ice Age, when the first crossings occurred, so much of the earth's water was impounded in polar ice caps or glaciers that the level of the oceans was lowered. This resulted in an isthmus connecting Siberia and Alaska. Even if these ancient hunters did not walk dry-shod over this spit of land, they certainly could easily have crossed over on the winter ice. In historical times, there was considerable contact and interchange between Eskimos on the Alaskan side and the Siberian side.

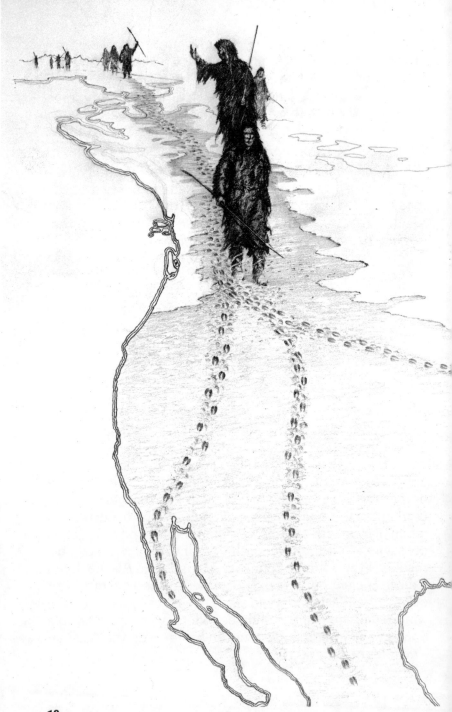

Various animals, many of which are extinct today, also made this crossing. Indeed, it was primarily the wanderings of such animals that lured these early nomadic hunters into the New World — not pioneering zeal. It should be emphasized that there was not just a single isolated crossing of Bering Strait by a group of humans. Rather, there were successive waves of human beings over a period of perhaps several thousand years.

These primitive hunters, after reaching the New World, travelled through the Yukon and Mackenzie River valleys, followed coast-lines and sought mountain passes.

The earliest inhabitants of North America crossed the Bering Land Bridge from Siberia and followed game trails through the ice-free corridor to lands in the south.

The continental ice sheet, a great glacier that spanned North America from sea to sea and stretched a thousand miles to the south, presented an imposing barrier to early migrants in their southward movement. Miraculously, there did remain an ice-free corridor, almost as if designed as a migratory aid to lands in the south. Actually, two separate ice sheets mantled the northern latitudes. The Laurentide Ice Sheet covered most of Canada east of the Rocky Mountains. A much smaller ice sheet, the Cordilleran, centered on the Rockies, and spread westward to the Pacific. The corridor formed between these ice sheets must have been an inhospitable area with its icy winds, driving snow, and frequent blinding fogs. Still, grazing animals entering the corridor would have been sufficient stimulus to lure these brave hunters onward. Eventually man inhabited most of the North American and South American continents. French prehistorian Francois Bordes has noted that not until man occupies another planet will he have such a vast virgin domain to explore. No special instinct guided the travels of primitive man, nor was there any particular reason why their migration was in a general southward direction. In fact, these hunters' ancestors initially had traveled generally northward to reach the Bering Land Bridge from Siberia. The only direction the early hunters followed was that of the game trails that lured them on at random; no doubt some bands even followed game trails that wandered back to Asia. Beyond the present trail there was always the horizon with its possibility of better hunting and perhaps a milder climate.

The Stone Age hunters who pursued the giant land mammals of their day are referred to by archaeologists as "Paleo Men," and their period in time is called the "Paleolithic Period." This is in contrast to the "Archaic Culture" and "Archaic Period" that includes the more modern Indians and Eskimos. The period of transition between the two cultures was very gradual, but for reference purposes has been arbitrarily set at 4000 B.C. The main factor bringing about this transition was the extinction of the giant land mammals which necessitated a whole new means of existence — one based more on gathering and later on horticulture.

How the Paleo Hunters existed has been laboriously pieced together from shreds of archaeological evidence, and much of their way of life still remains clothed in romantic supposition. The ancient hunter wore robes of fur, probably knew the use of fire, and carried stone-tipped spears to even the odds against the huge mammoths and other game he hunted.

To Stone Age hunters, the pursuit of big game was almost a form of warfare, where the hunted animal was an adversary whose death was necessary for the hunters' survival. Failure to kill these behemoths meant that privation and death would certainly follow. Stone Age big game hunting was a risky business, and the tables could turn rapidly, with the hunter suddenly becoming the hunted.

The animals primitive man hunted were the hairy and imperial mammoths, ancient camels and horses, sabre-toothed tigers, the long-horned bison (*Bison antiquus*), which was an ancestor of our American Bison (*Bison bison*) and rarely the flat-skulled mastodon. These animals were colossal; the commonly hunted mammoth stood more than thirteen feet (4 meters) at the shoulders and carried sixteen-foot (5 meter) tusks. The mammoth was a herbivore, and at one time grazed over most of the North American Continent.

Paleo hunters lived, hunted, and traveled in small bands of family groups. For the most part, they camped in the open and did not show the preponderance for cave dwelling that their European ancestors did, although there were exceptions. Camp would be made where game

The sabre-toothed cat, now extinct, was hunted by paleo men.

animals fell and when the meat was gone, or no longer good, they would move on. The main occupation these hunters engaged in, perhaps the only one they even knew about, was the grim business of survival through hunting.

As hunters, Paleo Men were opportunists in the most extreme sense. They would patiently skirt the perimeter of a herd, as did other predators, waiting for the right moment when a strayed calf or a weak adult would become

The long-horned bison *(Bison antiquus)* **was an ancestor of our present American bison** *(Bison bison).*

A group of Paleo hunters subdue a mammoth with spears and stones.

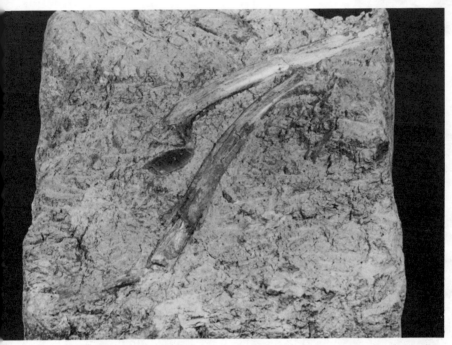

During an excavation in 1927, this Folsom point was found in situs among the bones of the now extinct *Bison antiquus figginsi* **in New Mexico. The landmark discovery extended our knowledge of man in the New World by several thousand years.**

separated, and could be ambushed. Natural traps such as boggy waterholes were taken advantage of to limit the movements of a flustered or wounded animal, and thus make the kill easier. Death would come slowly to such large animals, and it would take repeated spear thrusts and pounding with rocks and clubs to complete the task. When traveling through mountainous country, Paleo Man never failed to check fresh snow slides or avalanches where there would be a good chance of game being entrapped and frozen.

These first hunters left few traces of their ways of life. Human remains are almost non-existent; what few fragments have been discovered have posed more questions than they have provided answers. We know of these hunters mainly from their distinctively-shaped stone spear points that have been found with the bones of some of the long-extinct mammals. The dates of existence of many early land mammals are fairly well documented, and spear points, when found in association with them, can be similarly dated. One of the earliest and most famous discoveries of points unearthed with a "kill" made by a Paleo hunter occurred near Folsom, New Mexico in 1926. A cowboy, out looking for strays in a steep-walled arroyo, happened to notice a few old bones sticking out of an eroded bank. Poking curiously among these bones, he found a strange-looking, slender, fluted spear point. This chance discovery produced for the scientific community the bones of twenty-three long-horned bison and several fluted points later named Folsom in honor of the nearby town. The beasts had been driven into a box canyon with no avenue for escape, killed, and butchered.

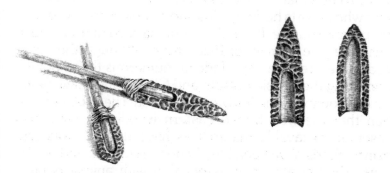

Folsom points characterized by their distinct flake scar are among the earliest spear tips used by man on the North American Continent.

It has been accurately stated that the greatest portion of the history of human existence on earth is written in flint and bone. The lot of the archaeologist has been to tease from an unrelenting earth shreds of evidence buried beneath the sediment of ages, and to painstakingly piece this history together.

Folsom and Clovis points are the earliest of ancient spear tips. The Clovis type probably predates the Folsom type, and is shaped somewhat differently. Both Folsom and Clovis points are amazingly well formed and technically advanced for such an early time in pre-history. They are fluted on each face, presumably to better fit the spear shaft. Depending on the locale, agate, chalcedony or flint were favored materials. Points were formed by a method known as pressure chipping — a rather unexpected technology for this early date. Fortunately, from an archaeological standpoint, Clovis and Folsoms are quite distinctive in form with their flute or flake scar running from the base partway to the tip. The unique appearance of these points has made them readily identifiable, a characteristic which has aided in their being traced all the way to the backdoor of the New World — the area around Bering Strait in Alaska.

Each discovery of a rare Folsom or Clovis point, be it by a professional archaeologist or by a casual weekend hiker who reports his find, adds another piece to a large and complicated puzzle. It should be emphasized that the West is not the sole domain of Paleo Man, although the most productive sites are here. Indeed, numerous fluted points resembling the classic Folsom and Clovis types have been found throughout the Midwest and East. The problem has been that the wet, humid eastern woodlands have not preserved decayable material as have the dry, western deserts. Finds have been largely on the surface, and not in undisturbed strata or in association with animal bones. Still, the inference that must be drawn from the finding of these midwestern and eastern fluted points is that Paleo

Man eventually spanned our continent from coast to coast.

The best estimates are that the first crossings into the New World occurred about 40,000 years ago or sooner. Folsom points found in New Mexico have been dated at 15,000 years of age. Thus, it is not illogical to deduce from these dates that the gradual southward migration of these people took 25,000 years to occur. Their progress was undoubtedly sporadic. Movement within each ecological zone might have been fairly fast. Encountering a new zone, however, would have entailed a slowing of the migratory spread to allow new adaptive patterns and survival techniques to evolve. This pattern can be seen in the Eskimos who were relative late-comers on the North American scene arriving about 6,000 years ago. They rapidly inhabited the entire Arctic coastline from Alaska to Greenland. So swiftly did this spread of inhabitation occur that their language did not experience regional variations and remained virtually the same across the top of the world.

Man came to North America during a period referred to as the Pleistocene on the paleontological time table. More commonly called the Ice Age, this was the period when the great land mammals roamed the continent. By now, the dinosaurs had long been extinct for reasons still not completely understood, although climatic changes may have been responsible for the demise of these awesome behemoths.

The ice age was a time of heavy rainfall, and the land of the Paleo hunters was dotted with lakes and ponds. As the glaciers retreated to the north, these lakes which had been fed by the glacial melt dried up, and the country became quite arid. Unlike the dinosaurs that preceded him, and even the large land mammals that he hunted, man, with his superior intelligence, was able to adapt — and to survive.

Eskimo with polar bear State Historical Society of Wisconsin

Hunters of the Ice

At minus 50 degrees F. (-46° C.), unprotected human flesh will freeze in three to four minutes. Initially, the cold causes an anesthetic-like numbness that allows freezing to occur without pain — and without warning. The agony that may have been spared in the freezing however, is unleashed in the process of thawing. A reddening of the skin is accompanied by an intense burning sensation, and as the thawing becomes complete there is swelling with excruciating pain. In a few hours, as the tissue dies, huge bullous blisters form and these rupture and leave grotesque, ulcerated areas that set the stage for the gangrene that follows. Even if frostbitten fingers are saved or a patch of skin heals with a scar tissue covering, the punishment of frostbite has just begun. For the remainder of the victim's life, this lesion will exhibit a tendency to recurrent frostbite, and the heightened sensitivity to cold will continue to cause torment. Such extreme cold is common in the arctic, and if a minus 50 degree F. (-46° C.) reading is fanned by just a 15 mile (24 kilometer) per hour "breeze," the windchill equivalent drops to an ominous minus 100 degrees F. (-73° C.). But to the Eskimos, who live on this frozen edge of the earth, the pain of frostbite is inconsequential. It signifies that they are alive; only death is painless.

The home of the Eskimo, the Arctic, is on the geographic limits of the area of our planet capable of supporting human life. That man can survive at all in this implacable land is a tribute to the human race, but that Eskimos are one of the most remarkably successful divisions of mankind is truly astonishing.

Traversing the North American continent from the tropics to the Arctic would show man's reliance on vegetable matter in the south giving way to an increasing dependence on animal matter farther north. The Eskimos, who live farthest north, represent the epitome of hunting cultures. Totally dependent on killing animals to survive, they are, so to speak, suprapredators.

The Arctic has a cruel climate — in July the mean temperature is 50 degrees F. (10° C.). The portion of the Arctic inhabited by Eskimos starts on the shores of the Chuckchi Peninsula in Siberia, crosses Bering Straits to the north slope of Alaska, extends through the Canadian Archipelago, includes the coast of Labrador, and ends on the east shores of Greenland.

The Arctic is a harsh but majestic land of haunting beauty. Just as there is perpetual sunlight in the summer, giving rise to the phrase "land of the midnight sun," the sun also disappears for an equal length of time in the winter causing a season of perpetual darkness. Even the summer sun is impotent at this latitude where it never climbs far above the horizon, and offers little warmth. Over most of the Arctic the average mean temperature is above freezing for only a little more than three months. Cold air has a lower saturation point for water vapor than does warm air, causing one of the driest climates on earth.

The Eskimos

The Eskimoan people came from Siberia about 6000 years ago. The tool remains that have been discovered, as well as present day Eskimo mythology, suggest that these wanderers were originally an inland culture and had not yet shown the inclination towards coastal living that was to be so crucial to their descendants. A division of these people migrated to the Aleutian Islands of Southwest Alaska, becoming Aleuts. Their culture exhibited considerable dependence on sea mammal hunting, which was perhaps a vestige of their Eskimo ancestry, although even more Northwest Coast influence was present. The Aleut's language, however, remained essentially Eskimoan. Of the remaining newcomers from Siberia, a few developed a coastal existence on the shore of the Bering Sea and the rest struck out across the tundra of interior Alaska and Canada. Known as the Denbigh or "Arctic Small Tool" Culture, these people traversed the top of the North American continent. Strong resistance was met from the Indians in the Canadian interior and the Denbigh People were pushed north to the Arctic coasts. Here, around 600 B.C., perhaps initially in the area of Foxe Basin in northern Hudson Bay, lifestyles and implements underwent an adaptation to an ice-hunting culture. Archaeologically, this era is recognized as the Dorset Culture.

These people were distinctly Eskimoan. Eskimos call themselves *Inuit*. This means, naturally, "the people." The word *Eskimo* is an Algonquin term meaning "eaters of raw meat." This is now a somewhat out-of-date term and most present-day Eskimos prefer to be called Inuit. In this text, the two terms will be used interchangeably.

Some Eskimos stayed in the Canadian Interior and were not forced to the arctic coasts. These people never abandoned their inland hunting techniques and continued to live primarily off the caribou. We refer to them as the Inland or Caribou Eskimos but they called themselves the *Ihalmiut*. Literally, this means "the other people" and by this title they distinguished themselves from the Inuit or "the people" who took up a coastal existence.

Although the Dorset Culture flourished and spread both east and west across the Arctic, it was destined to become extinct. About 1000 A.D., in the area of Point Barrow, Alaska, a more advanced culture based on the hunting of whales and other sea mammals developed. Named the Thule Culture after the region of Thule, Greenland, where its distinctive artifacts were first discovered, this was a relatively prosperous and vigorous lifestyle that soon spread along the entire Arctic Coast and back across Bering Straits to the ancestral homeland of Siberia. The Thule Culture spread in the east from Ellesmere Island, across Davis Straits, to both coasts of Greenland. Eskimos of the Thule Culture lived in permanent villages of 200-300 people and developed the technology to become masters of marine hunting.

Stone men, or *inukshuks,* **dot the arctic tundra lands of the Eskimo. Their purpose is unknown.**

The rapid spread of expertise and technology across 5000 miles (8,000 kilometers) of Arctic from Siberia to Greenland may seem incredible, but the smooth winter ice on the protected waters of the Beaufort Sea and the Canadian Archipelago was a regular thoroughfare for dog sleds. In 1976, the Japanese adventurer, Naomi Uemura, completed a 7,500-mile (12,070 kilometer) dog sled trip from Jakobshavn, Greenland to Kotzebue, Alaska in 18 months. Even the Eskimo language, essentially unchanged from Siberia to Greenland, is evidence of rapid cultural interplay among arctic peoples.

The elite Thule Culture in the 18th century waned also. Whale hunting, the mainstay of Thule Culture villages, disintegrated for reasons that are not certain. The decimation of whales by European whaling fleets may have been the cause, or the "Little Ice Age" that occurred about this time may have changed the habits of whales. Regardless of the reason, abandonment of village living and the dispersement into small nomadic groups along the coast resulted. This is the style of existence that characterized the modern phase of Eskimo life.

Surprisingly, the Eskimos were the first inhabitants of the New World to experience European contact. Norse seamen discovered people of the Dorset Culture on Greenland and Baffin Island around 850 A.D. The Norsemen called the Eskimos *Skraellings*, but, except for establishing themselves in Eskimo mythology and folklore, their impact was minimal.

Their inhospitable land protected the Eskimos from the debauching influence of the whites for more years than any other North American natives. Serious ethnographic research never got underway in North America until the late 1800's, and by this time acculturation had irrevocably altered the means of existence of most Indian groups. Only the hunting-oriented life of the Eskimo was preserved, relatively unaltered, for scientific investigation. Additionally, it is fortunate that many of the early arctic explorers — men like Knud Rasmussen, Peter Freuchen, Vilhjalmur Stefansson, Fridtjof Nansen, Kai Birket-Smith and Dr. Franz Boas — were not only astute observers of Eskimo life, but were also prolific chroniclers.

Eskimos lived in hunting groups or bands, and while they might have identified with others in certain geographic locations, there was no formal tribal recognition. The ending *"miut"* meant "the people of," and they simply added this suffix to place-names to identify themselves. Examples are the Kangramiut, the Ailvilingmiut, and the Nunivagmiut. Ethnologists have assigned collective terms to these groups on a geographic basis. The Western Eskimo group consists of the Chuckchi Eskimos of Siberia, all Alaskan Eskimos and the Mackenzie Eskimos of the Mackenzie River Delta area in the Yukon and the Northwest Territory. The Central Eskimos include most groups of the Canadian Archipelago. These are the Copper Eskimos to the west in the area of Coronation and Queen Maude Gulfs, the Netsilik Eskimos of the Eastern Canadian Arctic, the Inland or Caribou Eskimos of the Interior, and the Labrador Eskimos along the coastal areas of that province. The Eskimos farthest to the east are the Greenland Eskimos. These people live on both the east and west coasts of this continent-sized island. The northwest shore of Greenland is home for the Polar Eskimos who live farther north than any other group of people in the world. This band of 200 was "discovered" in 1818 by Sir John Ross, and so great was their isolation that they thought themselves, prior to the Ross Expedition, to be the only people on earth.

The Eskimoan language, though harsh and guttural sounding, carries many subtle nuances of meaning. The vocabulary content is an accurate reflection of their way of life. There is no word for art per se, nor for luck. Nonetheless, there are over 100 words for snow — defining precise shades of distinction in color, stickiness, depth, consistency, age, etc. There are as many, possibly more, words describing various ice conditions.

Snow and ice, though alien and hostile to modern man in his mechanized world, were true allies of the Eskimo. They allowed efficient transportation, provided building materials capable of giving warmth through insulation, and made the Eskimo's hunting techniques practical. The Eskimo's dome-shaped snow houses, or igloos, were architectural masterpieces of efficiency.

The igloo became the enduring hallmark of all polar peoples in the minds of most Euro-Americans because of the popular writings of many early English and Scottish explorers. Actually, only Eskimos of Canada's central and eastern Arctic used igloos, and then only in winter. Caribou skin-covered tents were used through the summer by all Eskimo groups.

Smithsonian Institution — Photo by Vilhalmur Stefansson or George H. Wilkins 1913-1918

A hastily constructed igloo serves as an admirable overnight shelter on a hunting trip in the central Arctic.

An Eskimo man and his wife from the Hudson Bay region are about to add an ice pane window as a finishing touch to their igloo. (1930)

In building an igloo, the ivory snow knife was used to draw a circle in the snow cover, outlining the floor. Trapezoid-shaped snow blocks were then cut from within the confines of the circle to build the igloo. The area from which the blocks were removed served as the sunken interior of the dwelling. It was important that the snow cover, or drift, from which the blocks were taken be from a single storm, else they would fall apart. These snow blocks were then laid in an ascending, inwardly leaning spiral: one person on the inside supporting the upper blocks as they were added by his companion on the outside. The final keystone-shaped piece of snow in the top center served as the linchpin that allowed all the blocks to become self-supporting as a unit. Snow shavings cut from the blocks to get a tight fit were then scooped up and used to chink the cracks. The final touch was a hole cut in the side for the insertion of a translucent piece of seal mesentery, or freshwater ice, to serve as a window. During times of the year when the sun was shining, this would be placed on the side of the igloo to get the greatest benefit from the sun's rays. A little reflecting shelf of snow might have been added at the proper angle to enhance the Arctic sun's effect, which even at midsummer only skirted the horizon. It was one of the first uses of solar energy. The entrance to the igloo faced south, away from the prevailing winds, and was in the form of a tunnel-covered trench. Snow benches built inside the igloo were used for tables and as beds. Keeping the living area above the entrance-way gained maximum benefit from the fact that warm air rises to the top of the igloo. Two Eskimos working together could complete an igloo in a little over an hour. If the snow house was located near a food cache made in the fall, or close to a good winter sealing area, it would be made more permanent than just an overnight shelter. This was accomplished by suspending the caribou skins from the summer tent inside the igloo by lines that extended through the snow wall and were toggled on the outside.

The interior of the igloo was lighted and heated by a dish-shaped lamp carved from soapstone. Originally used in the ancestral lands of Asia, no other lamps, except these of soapstone used by Eskimos, were found among any prehistoric culture of North America. Though their shelters may have been temporary, their soapstone lamps were prized as the symbol of their home at any location. Women, who customarily tended the lamps, prided themselves in their ability to keep the flame burning at an appropriate level for the cooking or heating chore at hand. A piece of frozen blubber was hammered to a mushy consistency and placed along the back of the lamp. Dry moss, twisted into a strand, was laid along the front edge of the lamp and ignited. The blubber, melted by burning the wick, was soaked up in the moss and fed the smokeless flame. As the interior of the igloo was heated by the lamp to a pleasant warmth, the inner wall would melt slightly. The melted water would not drip on the occupants, but rather run down the concavity of the igloo interior to refreeze and further solidify the structure.

Semi-subterranean sod house at Nushagak Village in Alaska. This was the type of dwelling most characteristic of the Western Eskimo.

The snow benches that were used for beds were covered with caribou hides. The first layer of skin would be for insulation and would have the hair-side down. The next layer would have the hair-side up in order to be next to the skin, and the Eskimo family would sleep together to pool their warmth beneath yet another caribou skin used as a blanket. Suffering from the cold inside a shelter was probably greatest in the spring. During this season, the daytime sun would start melting the roof of the igloo, yet it would still turn very cold at night. The caved-in roof would be covered with caribou skins, and the family would eagerly await further warming when they could forsake this half snow-half skin house and pitch their skin tents on the Arctic tundra.

"Iglu," in Inuit means "house." This was also the term applied to the abode of the Western Eskimo which, though similar in design to the dome-shaped snow houses of the Canadian Eskimo, was constructed of different material. These dwellings were more permanent and reflected the greater stability that was derived from hunting the larger sea mammals off the Alaskan coast. These dwellings were semi-subterranean and a foundation of piled stones supported rafters of either drift wood or whale bone. This framework supported a sod covering. Like the snow igloos, the passageway was partially underground which, besides being handy for storage, helped to conserve heat.

Man, being an essentially hairless species needed to depend upon the insulating qualities of the skins of other mammals for survival in the Arctic. More than any other animal, the caribou met these needs for the Inuit. The club-shaped configuration of their hair shafts was efficient in trapping air. In addition, air cells were located at the bulbous tips of the hairs and even further enhanced the insulating qualities of caribou skin. Typical winter attire consisted of two suits of caribou skin clothing. Their total weight was 10 pounds (4.5 kilograms). The inner suit would have the fur turned in against the skin while the outer suit had the fur on the outside. Just as in the construction of their igloos, the phenomenon of warmer air rising was faultlessly incorporated into the design of clothing. Both pants and parkas (an Eskimo invention) were kept baggy at the bottom to allow freedom of movement and to trap more air, but both were tied tightly at the top to prevent the escape of air warmed by the body. Sometimes pants were made of polar bear skin. The concept of layered clothing not only trapped more insulating air but also allowed outer garments to be shed during exertion or in warmer weather. Seal skin was preferred for jackets and trousers during times of increased precipitation in spring and summer because of greater water repellancy. Bird skins were sewn together for undergarments.

The tough hide of the bearded seal was used for the soles of boots. To this was sewn a caribou hide upper for winter wear or one of sealskin if intended for summer use. Boots were sewn with sinew which would swell when moistened and make the seam watertight. Arctic hare skins were fashioned into soft socks. A cushion of dried grass, gathered during the summer specifically for this purpose, was worn between the boots and the hareskin socks. This permitted the evaporation of moisture which would freeze if allowed to accumulate. Each night, the Eskimo wife would carefully inspect the boots for any needed repairs and change the grass liner. The wife might also chew the tough bearded seal soles until pliant so her husband could hunt in greater comfort. Among Eskimo men, it was the sewing capability of their wives that was boasted of more than looks, cooking ability, sexual prowess or any other attribute. Without a wife to perform such duties, a man was destitute. Only with clothing properly made and repaired by such a wife could an Eskimo be a successful provider in this severe environment.

Accumulation of moisture within clothing could not be tolerated as it would immediately freeze and the garments would lose most of their insulating properties. Even if there were not fresh snow, blowing snow was ever-present, therefore a stick was always conveniently left in the entranceway to beat this snow off the clothing before entering the warm interior. Once inside the house, clothes were immediately shed and hung to dry from caribou antler pegs near the top of the igloo. This also afforded the opportunity to pick the pesky lice from clothing. Inside the dwelling the family lived essentially in the nude, sprawling across the caribou skin blankets. The wife went about her inside chores scantily clad in perhaps a pair of fox-skin panties. The Eskimos unlike many whites, never felt ashamed of nudity.

After the passing of the Thule Culture, with its traditionally village-based lifestyle, Eskimos lived in small, highly mobile groups scattered widely over the Arctic. Although favorite hunting and fishing sites were used seasonally year after year, there were few permanent villages established in the post Thule era. The Eskimos became seasonal nomads. If an especially large catch of game were made, it was often more practical to relocate the entire camp to the kill site than to carry the bulky cache back to a distant village. Efficient means of transportation were important to such wanderers. The self-sufficient bands of Inuit scattered themselves along the arctic coasts.

In the north, there are two separate habitats: the land and the sea. Each was extensively used by the Eskimos in their hunting and fishing existence, and transportation over both realms was a necessity. To fully utilize the environment to their benefit, the village-based Thule people, as well as the earlier Dorset Eskimos, needed mobility across both land and ocean. That the sea can exist in either frozen or open-water states provided an additional variable. This blending of land and the frozen or open surface of the ocean makes up one of the earth's most unique environments.

Sea ice itself is never static, but rather is in a constant state of flux. Wind and ocean current are the prime determinants of ice movement. The vagaries of these elements are less evident on the more sheltered seas of the Canadian Archipelago or within the fjords of Greenland than they are along the Alaskan and Siberian coasts. On the unbuffered seas of northwest Alaska, wind and current create havoc with the frozen surface. Great cracks, or leads, are suddenly ripped open and as these are slammed back together the momentous force causes rafting and piling of the ice — creating a nightmarish jaggedness making traveling difficult. Along these unprotected coasts most long distance travel is done on the ice foot that extends for a short distance from shore.

The behavior of sea ice had to be intimately understood not only for safety in traveling upon it, but also for success in locating game on and around it. New ice does not build up along the shore, gradually thickening and extending itself as the season progresses. Rather, the ice pack forms far out at sea and is carried to the land by an onshore wind or current.

In no other geographic location are clues to the environment more subtle or more important than on the arctic ice. A shade of difference in the color of ice, miniscule changes in the consistency or surface drift patterns of snow, or light reflected from pack ice onto a layer of clouds: each of these was encyclopedic in the information they contained for the Eskimos. A low layer of clouds frequently would hang over the interposition of land and sea in the Arctic and light reflected by the earth's surface against these clouds created a "sky map." A dark band of cloud cover over the pack ice indicated that an open lead was below. This condition was called a "water sky." A milky white sky reflected light from solid pack ice, and was referred to as an "ice blink."

The color of the ice itself is the most important indicator of safe or unsafe ice. Rotten or unsafe ice is characteristically very dark, and varying shades of gray become increasingly safer as the color lightens. The extensive fields of flat, unpiled ice in Canada and Greenland are more protected and a deeper snow covering accumulates on this "lagoon ice." Such a covering of snow negates the usually reliable indicators of ice color and Eskimos of these areas relied more heavily on their dogs, who would instinctively shy away from unsafe ice.

Offshore leads may vary from a few feet to several miles in width and they may remain open for weeks or may close within a few hours. As the great Russian authority on sea ice, Nikolai Zubov, has noted, the presence of a lead is more directly dependent on the forces of wind or current than on temperature or season. These leads, caused by the movement of ice, were extremely bountiful with marine mammals. The Western Eskimos of Alaska hunted extensively along these fertile open leads that usually ran parallel to the shore.

The greatest danger of ice hunting was being cast adrift on an ice floe that had severed its bond with the landfast ice and became free to move and drift with the current. The limits of human endurance and survival capabilities have been tested in terrible ordeals when Eskimo hunters were trapped for days on these ice floes. Even though landfast ice might have been only a few tantalizing yards away, to plunge into the icy sea water meant certain death from freezing. The Eskimos' only recourse was to try to endure the cold and hunger until their ice prison abutted solid ice onto which they could cross. Such hunters, ravaged by starvation, ate their boots and harpoon lines in a desperate bid to survive. One Polar Eskimo, according to Knud Rasmussen, after eating his boots, amputated his own frozen feet and ate them for what nourishment they might afford since they were useless to him frozen. The dangers of being stranded on the ice were indelibly etched in the minds of Eskimos, and they treated the ice edge with great respect. A lead, regardless of how narrow, was never crossed if there was an offshore wind or current or the possibility of one arising. When conditions prevailed that might push the pack farther offshore, hunting was done only from the landfast edge of the lead unless the hunters had a boat with them.

An Alaskan Eskimo with his sled and dog team harnessed in tandem.

Dog sled was the preferred means of transportation across the winter ice of the Arctic. Although style and technique differed from one location to another, the sled and dog team was ubiquitous among the Eskimos. Available materials dictated the construction of sleds. Driftwood was the only wood of substantial enough size available to the Eskimos for sled building and therefore was the favored material. In some areas, such as the Gulf of Boothia inhabited by the Polar Eskimos, driftwood was so scarce that these people thought the paltry amounts they did occasionally find grew on the floor of the ocean. Actually, these pieces of wood probably floated down Siberian rivers and then drifted across the polar basin. An unintentional gift from whaling crews in the post-contact era was the flotsam of several hundred ships known to have been wrecked in arctic waters. Timber from some of these ships was the first driftwood to ever reach some arctic shores and was a windfall to Eskimos of those areas. After the wood was procured, sleds were lashed together with sealskin thongs which gave them the flexibility to sustain pounding trips across rough ice.

National Museum of Canada, Ottawa

A Western Eskimo ices his sled runners. Arctic fox skins hang in the background.

If they did not have the luxury of a supply of driftwood for sled construction, the Eskimos used whale bone, caribou antler, or walrus tusk ivory. The best sleds were made of whale baleen runners with driftwood crossbars. Thick, gooey mud was collected in balls during the fall and frozen to be manufactured into sled runners. Later, in the warmth of the igloo, these were thawed and molded into the proper shape and set outside to freeze. A glazing of ice was necessary on the surface of these mud runners, as well as those made of other materials, to permit them to glide smoothly over the frozen surface. This thin coating of ice was formed by taking a mouthful of water, skillfully spewing it over the surface of the runners, allowing it to rapidly freeze, and repeating the procedure until the entire surface of both runners was glazed. If while traveling a re-icing of the runners became necessary and no fire was available to obtain melted water from snow, a carefully directed stream of urine sufficed. Usually several bladdersful were required and even women, if they were traveling in the groups, were obliged to squat unceremoniously over the sled runner and make their contribution.

Adequate emergency sleds were fabricated from seal, caribou or walrus hides rolled into long narrow cylinders. These were dipped through a hole in the ice until thoroughly soaked and then formed into the up-turned shape of runners as they froze solid. A mud and ice coating was applied to each runner and frozen fish or strips of frozen walrus meat were lashed into place as cross members. If not very good looking, such a sled was at least serviceable and offered the extra advantage of being able to be thawed and eaten if the need arose.

Harnessing techniques for dog teams differed in the eastern Arctic from those in the west. The Siberian, Alaskan, and MacKenzie Eskimos of the west employed the tandem style of harnessing with two dogs abreast. Teams would vary in the number of dogs from two to a dozen, depending largely on the amount of dog food available and, to a lesser extent, on how many dogs had to be killed in lean times and eaten as emergency rations. The strongest dogs were used as wheel dogs and harnessed directly in front of the sled. The smartest and most spirited member of the dog team was used as a lead dog and it was hoped that its efforts would be an inspiration to the rest of the team. Occasionally, a bitch in heat was harnessed into the lead dog position since the male members were sure to strive to follow her. Less well-behaved dogs were kept close to the rear of the team to be less of a distraction and also to be more easily reached with the whip. On the smooth ice of Greenland and the Canadian Archipelago, where narrow passages between ice hummocks were less of a problem, dogs were harnessed fan style: each dog pulling its own trace attached to the sled and the whole team operating abreast.

At rest, a dog team was a chaotic collection of quarreling animals and tangled traces. Once in motion however, the team and sled became as one as the skilled Eskimo driver adjusted to the conditions at hand. The sled was trimmed and the dogs controlled with quick almost imperceptible motions and calls. Each dog had its own peculiar traits, and these idiosyncrasies were well understood and appropriately dealt with by the driver. Indeed, on a long trip they became the amusement and diversion of the Eskimo hunter out on the ice. Some dogs learned to keep their lead lines tight without really pulling while others always tried to veer toward the easier snow. Occasionally some dogs developed the habit of dropping back from their position to relieve themselves whenever the pulling became particularly strenuous. Furthermore, one of the greatest indignities to be suffered by the Eskimo hunter was to have his team bolt and take off with an empty sled while his attention was diverted. Sleds left momentarily unattended while scouting for game were turned over so the tips of the runners would dig into the ice and check the escape of the dogs.

Descended from wolves, Eskimo sled dogs were a

study in hardiness. It was their lot, even on the coldest of nights, to curl up on the ice with their tail over their nose and ears and allow the snow to drift over them for insulation. They were fed fish and walrus in the summer and the heads, entrails and bones of seals in the winter. Even in times of abundance they were fed only every other day. Hungry dogs were fast dogs and the hardest day's pull could always be obtained from the animals on the day they were not fed. During moderately lean times sled dogs could go 8-10 days without food. Their appetites were perpetually voracious and harnesses, whips, harpoon lines and even skin-covered boats had to be kept out of their reach lest they be consumed. Grinding the dog's teeth down flat with an abrasive stone impaired their eating ability enough to only partially solve this problem.

A cherished morsel of food for starved Eskimo dogs was warm human exrement and their gluttonous manner of obtaining these tidbits created some rather distressing situations out in the open. If the biting cold wasn't enough for the Eskimo to endure while responding to the urge, then certainly a team of dogs crowding around made the task almost intolerable.

There was some relief if the hunter was not alone and his partner, whip in hand, could keep the dogs away. When leaving a temporary hunting shelter, the final task before harnessing the team was to use the igloo as a comfort station after which the eager dogs were allowed inside to "clean up."

On the spring seal hunts an additional problem was encountered with the dogs. Ice would melt during the increasingly warm days only to refreeze at night in the form of small crystalline ice spicules that damaged the sled dog's feet. When these conditions existed the dogs were made to wear sealhide booties for protection. The animals intensely hated these, but they soon learned that any attempt to chew them off meant a sound thrashing. Pads lacerated by ice or otherwise injured presented a danger because the pain would force the sled dogs to sleep with their legs outstretched rather than folded under their bodies. The result, predictably, was a frostbitten paw.

With the appearance of leads of open water in May and June, transportation by skin-covered boats became increasingly important. The kayak was primarily a hunting craft, perhaps the most efficient ever designed. These light and maneuverable, single-seat boats were universally used among Eskimos, except for the Polar Eskimos of northwest Greenland. That far north there was not enough driftwood from which kayak frames could be fashioned and, also, there was not really enough open water for the craft to be practical.

The fragmenting pack ice in the spring made the combination of a hand-pulled sled and kayak an effective duo to use for traversing the expanses of ice that were laced with numerous areas of open water. The light kayak was easily pulled on the sled over the ice, and when a lead was encountered, the sled could be carried on the foredeck as the kayak was paddled across the opening. Launching the kayak from an ice edge required a well-practiced maneuver. The hunter would straddle the cockpit as he pushed the craft out and then slip into the seat as the ice began to buckle. Boarding the easily-tipped kayak was still trickier in the summer after the ice apron had disappeared. Then the paddler had to step down from an ice hummock that was usually a few feet above the water level.

Open-water summer sealing from a kayak was an important means of providing food for Eskimos across most of the Arctic, particularly for obtaining the large bearded seal whose hide was necessary for boat covers. It was in Greenland however, that kayak design and use reached the pinnacle of perfection. The skilled kayaker could turn his agile craft bottom-side-up and then right-side-up again, all with a deft stroke of the double-bladed paddle. This practiced move not only afforded the means of righting a capsized kayak, but the craft could also be purposefully turned over if a large breaker was about to be met at right angles. Meeting a large wave head-on was likely to result in the kayaker having his spine broken as the breaker pounded across the foredeck of the craft, unless the capsizing maneuver was not skillfully carried out. With such a repertoire of skills together with capable crafts, Inuit hunters were undaunted by stormy seas. Indeed, they preferred rough water because a closer approach could be made to swimming seals under the cover of waves. The Eskimo and the interior of his kayak were protected from the frigid sea water by seal intestine parkas. The bottom of the parkas had a draw string that went over the cowling of the kayak to make it watertight when pulled taut and tied. Well-oiled seal intestine parkas were amazingly water-proof, and the sinew thread with which the overlapping pieces of intestine were sewn would swell when wet and make the seams watertight.

The large open umiaks that were up to 30 feet (9 meters) in length and required a crew of as many as twelve, were designed primarily for whaling. When whaling waned along with the Thule Culture, the umiak became more of a "woman's boat" and was used less as a hunting craft and more as transportation for families and their belongings from one coastal area to another. Just as there were no whales present in the Central Arctic, there were no umiaks among the Central Eskimos, although the crafts were well established among both the Alaskan and Greenland Eskimos.

Despite the rigors of the Arctic, Eskimos had a rich and full existence and were a happy people. They were generally optimistic and derived considerable pleasure from the few amenities that did exist in their harsh life. It was as if their capacity for gaiety and happiness were a form of psychological sublimation to keep them going in such a forbidding land. With incredible tenacity and ingenuity, they took snow and stone, ice and ivory, skin and bone, and flourished. The personal errors and near-disasters that occurred while hunting were made light of, and the Eskimos were quick to good-naturedly poke fun at themselves for their clumsiness. They were admirable in defeat and did not brood over failure or the resulting misfortunes. Even the gravity of severe hardships that resulted in accidental death or starvation were resignedly shrugged off. "Ayornamat," they would say, "It can't be helped." What might seem to modern society a blasé attitude toward life was in reality the total acceptance of the fact that life in their environment was precarious at best. With an attitude like this, the Eskimos psychologically prepared themselves to accept their hard existence, and even death, with equanimity.

In this implacable land they learned that the way of the reed was better than that of the oak. They exercised restraint, flexibility, caution or daring as the situation dictated. Risk was an everyday reality for these hunters of the northern ice. Armed with a thorough knowledge of every aspect of their environment, the Eskimo was prepared to discuss, and evaluate all alternatives to a dangerous task. They were a cautious people by nature and possessed an innate ability to calculate risk. Only when it was decided that the urgency of a situation called for a certain action to be taken regardless of the risk would the Eskimo hunter stoically proceed.

Living in a hostile realm such as the north, where emergencies, disasters and privation were common, fostered an air of cooperation among Eskimos. Even in the post-Thule era, when relatively permanent village life was abandoned in favor of dispersement into small hunting groups, an attitude of sharing prevailed. If, during lean times, only one hunter had some luck, there would at least be some food in camp, the successful hunter being expected to share. Certainly a dense population could not be supported in the Arctic, but several hunters in camp lessened the risk of starvation. Particularly during winter-sealing, partnerships were formed. In some instances, an Eskimo's hunting partner for life was chosen by his mother shortly after birth. Each hunting partner was assigned a particular part of a seal, and when the boy grew to manhood and began killing seals, his wife was careful to give the specified part of the butchered seal to the appropriate sharing partner. A hunting partner who received, for example, the right shoulder of a seal, was referred to by his hunting comrade as "my right shoulder."

Hunters were viewed as lucky or unlucky and were not labeled by their fellow Inuit as bad or inept. Still the fight for survival went on and there was no room for non-producers. Lazy hunters experienced group ostracism and ridicule and this was generally sufficient to get them back in line.

Survival in a land like the Arctic dictated a different set of values, a different way of thinking; a working of the mind that modern society has a very difficult time grasping. Concepts of discomfiture such as cold, wetness, hunger, and exhaustion are viewed entirely differently by Eskimos. It can be called "toughness," but such hardships are anticipated by these indomitable people, and they are mentally resigned to that fact and relatively unaffected by it.

The openness of the Arctic conveys a feeling of limitless expanses of distance and an infinity of time. Both these parameters were a vague and unimportant concept in the Inuit mind and white man's preoccupation with such dimensions mystified and annoyed them. They knew nothing of days or weeks, but concerned themselves only with seasons and how they affected their means of providing. The Inuit's only alarm clock was biological: they slept when tired, ate when hungry (if food was available), and much of the remainder of the time concerned themselves with whatever tasks survival required, regardless of

A Western Eskimo man prepares to leave on a hunting trip. A kayak and sled are in front of his sealskin-covered tent.

the time of day.

Blubber was indispensable for Eskimo survival in the Arctic. The lack of blubber meant cold dark igloos as there would be no oil to burn in the lamps. It also meant excruciating thirst as without blubber to burn there was no means of melting freshwater ice or snow to drink. Eating snow would only induce greater thirst. While caribou, muskoxen and other arctic land mammals have specialized fur to provide warmth from the extreme cold, aquatic mammals have a special problem. Water temperatures in the Arctic Ocean remain fairly constant at 28 degrees F.

(-2° C.) and this is usually considerably warmer than the air temperature. But, conduction of heat is approximately 250 times greater in water than in air. It is protection from heat loss, an insulating medium, that is needed by sea mammals and fat, or blubber, serves splendidly for this. As a food for man, blubber is rich in caloric content and fuels the Eskimo's high metabolic rate, which in turn generates warmth.

Seal Hunting

Seals are widely distributed over the Arctic and are usually quite abundant. They have classically been the most reliable food source available to Eskimos. In addition to blubber, they provided fresh meat and a hide which was used for clothing, harpoon lines, dog harnesses, boot covers, and a myriad of other uses. The skin of the ringed seal was preferred for clothing while the tough hide of the huge bearded seal (sometimes reaching seven feet |2 meters| in length and 800 lbs. |362 kilograms| in weight) was mostly used for boot soles, cordage, and kayak and umiak covers. To make a harpoon line, a bearded seal skin was staked out on the ground and a hole cut in the center. The Inuit were expert at cutting an unvarying finger wide strip starting at this center hole and progressing in an unbroken, concentric spiral until the skin was used up. The line was then stretched and dried.

Harbor seals required open water and were only seasonally available, while the ribbon seal was rare and its use inconsequential. The ringed seal, by far the most abundant and found throughout the Arctic in all seasons, was the real mainstay.

"It sleeps," Eskimos said of the land in winter, and they turned their attention to the frozen Arctic Ocean. Winter camps located on the frozen sea were warmer than a camp could be on land due to the moderating effect of the 28 degrees F. (-2° C.) sea water circulating under the ice pack. But more importantly, beneath this petrified ocean crust, the icy waters were filled with life. Near the top of the sub-ice food chain were seals, swimming beneath the ice-covering and feeding on fish and crustaceans. Seals, being mammals with lungs, must come to the surface to breathe. For this purpose they maintained a series of breathing holes through the pack ice. It was the predictability of seals returning to these vital vents to breathe that made possible the most productive and classic method of Inuit hunting. The seal, more than any other animal, sustained life for the Eskimo. Since early times, from Siberia to Greenland, but particularly in the central Arctic, these stoic hunters maintained their patient vigil, ignoring the intense cold and hovering with their harpoon over seal breathing-holes.

As ice began to form in the fall, seals used their sharp claws to scratch a hole from the underside of the ice through to the top. Sea ice can eventually attain a thickness of up to six feet (2 meters), too thick for a seal to form a new hole, so established vents had to be kept open by scratching away newly formed ice every time the seal visited its breathing hole. Each seal had a number of breathing holes, and considerable time elapsed before a given one was visited. Chances were increased by the fact that several seals used a single hole. Even though a lead might open up which the seals could freely use, they still had to maintain their breathing holes with occasional visits, for certainly the lead would eventually close.

Each breathing hole was surrounded by a characteristic doughnut-shaped formation on the surface of the ice. These were created by water sloshing out from the hole each time the seal came up and also from the frozen condensation, or rime, from the seal's breath. On new ice swept free of snow by the wind, these breathing holes were easily spotted. The lagoon ice of Canada and Greenland, however, usually had a fairly thick snow cover. The seal was able to breathe through the loose snow, but it made the holes almost impossible to find without the use of dogs trained to sniff them out.

After the breathing holes were located, it had to be determined if they were in use. Though a thin sheet of ice might cover the bottom of an active hole, it would be frozen solid if no longer being visited by seals. The musk gland of male seals began to reek quite noticeably as the breeding season approached in late winter and this odor could be detected even by the hunter if a male seal had recently visited the hole. The female, however, left no odor.

When the seal visited the hole, it was harpooned with a blind thrust into the center of the hole by the waiting hunter. Usually it struck somewhere about the head, hopefully in the upper lip as tough skin here held the harpoon-toggle securely. Seldom did the seal's breathing hole extend vertically through the ice covering, but instead usually tunneled in from the side. The intricacies and contortions of each hole had to be carefully probed by the ice pick on the butt of the harpoon so the direction of the seal's arrival could be determined. Only with such information could the thrust of the harpoon be properly angled to score a hit.

In areas of heavier snow cover, seal indicators were sometimes used. These were made of a long spicule of bone with a tiny sliver of baleen or the rib of a feather tied to it. These were struck in the snow cover over the hole and a quivering of the indicator would signify the presence of a seal in the hole. Seals are wary, however, and the less disturbance of the hole and the snow cover to alert the seal the better.

Breathing-hole hunting required much patience. While the seal might appear a few minutes after the hunter had positioned himself, more likely a cold wait of several hours was in store. The wait was made more of an ordeal because it had to be in complete silence. Even the muffled sound of a foot moving on the ice as the hunter shifted his weight could alert an approaching seal and ruin the entire hunt. Furthermore, the spooked seal wouldn't return to that hole for quite some time.

When positioning himself at the hole, the hunter would try to get as comfortable as possible. He would need to be downwind from the hole to not be detected by the seal when it arrived. The hunter would also try not to face the wind, and he might even build a screen of snow blocks for his protection. The snow that covers sea ice is perenially wet deriving its moisture from the salt ice beneath it. To avoid this moisture, the Inuit seldom sat directly on the surface without some kind of protection. Usually they perched on a small three-legged stool which offered the extra advantage of making the shadow of the hunter's feet less obvious from beneath the ice. As a minimal preparation, the hunter would spread a piece of skin by the hole to stand on in order to muffle sound and to offer some insulation from the cold.

The cavity in the ice pack beneath a seal breathing hole usually came up obliquely from the sea. This offered an ice ledge for the seal to rest on before making a final approach to the vent.

Muscle tremors became a problem for seal-hole hunters after remaining motionless for long hours in the cold. A solution was to tie their legs together with a thong containing on one end a buckle with two holes. One end of the thong was firmly tied to a hole in the buckle and the other end, after passing around the hunter's legs, ended in a knot that passed tightly through the second hole. The binding could be quickly opened with a strong effort by the hunter when a seal appeared.

During the wait, the hunter might draw one arm inside his caribou skin parka to conserve heat. An antler or ivory hook kept the sleeve in position so his arm could be quickly and quietly reinserted when the seal came. The harpoon was either held or kept ready on two pegs beside the hunter within easy reach. Likewise a snow knife, used to enlarge the hole to extract the seal after it was harpooned, was kept handy.

Not only was it important for the hunter to station himself downwind — for the first thing the seal would do upon arriving at the hole was to sniff the air for danger — but also, if the hunt were in daylight, the Eskimo had to make sure his shadow didn't fall across the hole. After the seal had tested the air and satisfied itself that no danger lurked at the breathing hole, it would scratch around briefly to clean the vent of newly formed ice. Then it would take several long, deep breaths, making a rather loud hissing sound. At this moment the Inuit hunter would plunge his harpoon with all his strength through the hole and hopefully into the seal. The harpoon shaft might quickly disengage from the tip and fall to the ice, or it might be pulled down through the hole which would only further impede the seal's struggles. The harpoon line was held with one foot while the hole was enlarged with the snow knife so the seal could be withdrawn.

Once out on the ice, the seal would usually be still alive. Graceful swimmers underwater, they are nearly

The hunter gets into position by a seal breathing hole.

helpless on land. The seal would be rolled over onto its back and the hunter would lift the head and upper part of its body off the ice. The neck was then sharply flexed toward the chest, and the full weight of the Eskimo was brought down on the seal until a loud snap sounded signaling that the neck vertabrae had been disarticulated and the spinal cord severed. As the seal died, a thong, or seal pull with an ivory handle, was attached to the seal to facilitate the pulling of the carcass back to camp. It might also have been loaded on a toboggan made of strips of whale baleen lashed together, the smaller ends turned up in front.

While the butchering of whales and walrus was traditionally done by men, seals were always processed by the women inside the igloo or subterranean house. Not surprisingly, this was attended with considerable ritual. A sprinkling of fresh snow was put on the igloo floor and, before the skinning could begin, fresh water was poured into the mouth of the slaughtered animal. They reasoned that since seals lived in salt water they must have always been thirsty, and by showing this respect the seal's spirit was appeased. In turn the animal would speak favorably of these people who had treated it honorably and other seals would have little reason not to be killed by the Inuit hunters. One of the strictest taboos was not spiritually separating land and sea mammals. An Inuit lady could not work on the carcass of a land mammal on the same day that she had on an aquatic mammal, and the two could never be cooked in the same pot.

A variation of seal-hole hunting is possible late in the winter when most of the snow has left the ice and the breathing holes are easily spotted. An attempt is made to locate every hole in a given area and someone is stationed at each of these. Even the women and children are recruited for this task. They will make noise on the ice at each of these holes. Only one hole, where the hunter with his harpoon is stationed, is left undisturbed, and it is here that, hopefully, the seal will visit for his breath of air. Another method of tilting the odds of a seal making an appearance at a given hole was by the hunter urinating a few drops at each hole to leave scent except where he was going to station himself.

Nets made of strips of hide, called babiche, were used to capture seals. One method, used where the ice was not too thick, was to suspend the nets parallel with the pack ice beneath a breathing hole. Holes were cut in the ice on four sides of a breathing hole a short distance from it. A weight suspended from one corner of the seal net was dropped through one hole and retrieved up through an adjacent hole by a stick with a hook on the end. The process was repeated for the other holes until the net hung suspended beneath the breathing hole. Each corner of the net was toggled to the ice surface. A seal coming to this breathing hole would become entangled in the net, drown and could be retrieved. Seals swimming in the water did not show the timidity that they did on or near the ice surface.

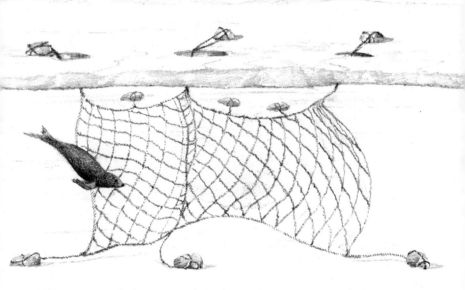

A babiche seal net is hung in curtain fashion beneath the ice parallel to an open lead.

Seal netting was most commonly done along open water leads usually off the Alaskan coast where strong ocean currents created more leads. In fact, the art of net-making died out completely in the central Canadian Arctic. These seal nets were suspended vertically, like a curtain, from the ice surface and would run parallel with the open water lead. A line in the middle of the net would be used to haul it up. Seals would congregate and frolic in the open leads but would periodically swim under the ice to maintain their breathing holes for when the lead closed. Sounds that might frighten a seal lying on top of the ice or approaching a breathing hole would actually serve to attract seals in the open water. Scratching noises seemed particularly enticing, and Eskimos fashioned "seal scratchers" from ivory or driftwood. Many of these sported real seal claws to supposedly enhance the effect. Used in slow rhythmic strokes with occasional pauses, these were effective in luring seals to the lead edge where nets were strung. Ice-edge netting was one of the more dangerous forms of hunting along the Alaskan Coast because leads were usually formed by strong currents, and ice conditions were often unstable under such forces. Not infrequently a patch of ice under a group of seal netters would be broken loose from land-fast ice and set adrift.

Seal scratchers made of ivory and driftwood typically sported real seal claws and were used to lure seals into nets suspended under the ice edge along open leads.

March is the breeding season for most arctic seals. They excavate dens in snow hummocks on the pack ice. These are 8-10 feet (2-3 meters) in length and have a diving hole at one end. Sometimes natural dens are formed within cavities of rough ice. Frequently, Eskimos used sled dogs to locate seal dens. The hunter would jump onto the roof, caving it in, and then try to block the retreat of the mother seal into the sea. Usually she escaped, but the awkward pups were taken by surprise. The baby seals were drawn out of the den by a special hook on the end of a long pole that twisted in their fur, and they were killed by stepping on their chest. Sometimes the mother could be lured back by tying a line to a hind flipper of one of the pups and throwing it down in the hole. Its pitiful cries often brought the mother out from under the ice where she was watching, in an attempt to rescue her pup. When she came, the hunter was ready with his harpoon. Arctic foxes also revel in hunting young seals and, although they will consume the carcass, they usually leave the skin behind. Such a skin discovered by an Inuit hunter is salvaged as a bonus find.

As the roofs of the pupping dens break down in the warmer rays of the early summer sun, the females can be seen with their pups basking beside their holes. The solitary male seals too, attracted by this warmth, crawl on the top of the ice to bask and sleep. Powerful and balletic in the sea, seals are awkward on the ice and must remain close to the sanctuary of their hole. As the sunless months of the arctic winter gradually gave way to the northward rush of spring and the 24 hour sunlight, a new form of seal hunting was practiced.

Two hunters traveling by dog sled searched for seals sunning on the ice. When a seal was spotted, one Eskimo remained behind to corral the dogs while the other started a diligent stalk over the ice towards the seal. The trick was to get within harpoon range — about ten paces. Solitary seals were preferred for the stalk since they were easier to approach than a group. One seal that was frightened would alarm the others in a group, and they would all slip off into the water. Of course, an approach from downwind was essential, and before the stalk was even begun the hunter would test the wind direction by plucking a hair from his seal coat and observing which way it fluttered to the ground.

The seal is a fitful sleeper while on the top of the ice, periodically looking up and glancing about to detect danger. The ice-stalking hunter had to synchronize his movements with the sleep of the seal, advancing only when the seal's head was down. The alert periods of a single seal seemed to be spaced between nearly identical sleep intervals, just as if tripped by some internal alarm clock. Furthermore, a muscular twitching of the sleeping seal, not unlike the skin contractions of a horse plagued by flies, occurs just before it awakens. Observation of this would alert the stalker that the seal's head was about to come up and that it was time to freeze. If the seal became uncomfortably suspicious, the hunter might allay its fears by imitating the seal's movements. The theatrics could become quite convincing as the hunter would roll over on his back in seal fashion and play with his hands and feet as a seal might his flippers. He might even make a blowing sound and scratch the ice to pacify the seal. The mimicry was further enhanced by the seal skin suit which the hunter wore. Once the seal became secure in the belief that it was truly another seal in the distance, it would stop watching the man and either go back to sleep or gaze off in another direction. Sometimes the ice-stalking seal hunter pushed a harpooning screen in front of him to hide his outline. In the Thule Greenland area these screens were made of bleached-white skin and in other regions a section of polar bear skin was used. Classically, these screens were mounted on small sleds which the hunter pushed in front of himself. Even blocks of snow were sometimes used. When the hunter was within range the harpoon was hurled, usually with the aid of a throwing board or atlatl.

Seals frolicking in the open leads were constantly stalked at the ice edge and harpooned but, as the season advanced and there was more open water, this was replaced by kayak hunting. The timidity exhibited by seals approaching a breathing hole or basking on an ice floe was replaced by the almost curious nature of swimming seals, and not infrequently they would willingly approach a kayak to within harpoon range. Inuit kayak hunters found that swimming seals preferred to congregate about some type of structure, an ice hummock or irregularity in the ice floe edge, and that straight, featureless ice edges were frequently unproductive.

The atlatl propelled seal spear gave greater power.

Seal spears were very light harpoons, and were usually thrown with atlatls since sitting in a kayak was a somewhat awkward position from which to throw. The harpoon was stored under a thong on the foredeck of the kayak where it was handy for fast action. The line was carefully coiled on a platform just in front of the manhole, and if an inflated seal skin float was attached to the end of the harpoon line, this was carried on the aft deck. Instead of seal skin floats, many of these small harpoons had inflated seal bladders tied directly to the shaft to increase drag on the seal as it towed the disengaged shaft after being harpooned. Other harpoon shafts were attached to the main line in such a way that they would be dragged through the water at right angles to the line of escape of the impaled seal. These shafts were stained red for better visability, and offered considerable resistance to the fleeing seal. The sudden ducking motion of the seal when initially struck almost always disengaged the tip of the harpoon, or toggle, from the shaft.

Denver Public Library — Western History Department Photo by Edward Curtis

Spring hunting paraphernalia: bird spears, seal harpoon, *atlatl,* **platform for coiled harpoon line, sled for crossing ice floes and a sealskin float.**

A Nunivak Eskimo from Western Alaska prepares to embark on an open-water sealing venture.

Winter seals had excessive amounts of blubber and this low-density substance made them extremely buoyant. Summer seals were less fat and they often sank after they were killed and then had to be retrieved by the harpoon line. If summer seals killed from a kayak were to be towed home behind the craft, provisions had to be made to make the carcass float. For this purpose slits were made in the skin at various points and a long pointed bone or ivory instrument was inserted to free the hide from the carcass around the opening. The hollow wing bone of a bird was then introduced through which air was blown and the space inflated. Carved wooden or ivory plugs were inserted to keep the air from escaping, and such a puffed-up seal would bob at the end of a line while being towed back to camp behind the kayak.

Walrus Hunting

It would be inconsistent for an animal the size of a walrus — those ungainly looking giants of the ice pans — to be overlooked by the enterprising Inuit. The ivory tusks furnished important material for making tools and the heavy mandible bone was used for some harpoon parts. The hide, particularly of the baby walrus, made good harpoon line and that of the adult was used to cover umiaks. Drum heads were made from the tough membrane that surrounded the liver. The organs and blubber were eaten but the meat was usually reserved for dog food unless times were particularly difficult. The flippers, however, were considered a delicacy after the chemistry of decay had heightened their taste some.

Though walrus spend their lives in close proximity to pack ice, they are essentially animals of open water, and this makes them available only on a seasonal basis. Like whales, they are able to open holes for breathing by bursting through the ice cover from below until it reaches a foot (.3 meters) in thickness and then they must move to an area of open water or thinner ice. Strong currents can keep isolated sections of frozen ocean open year-around. Called *polynyas*, these places might contain resident populations of non-migrating walrus. Their migration is somewhat a passive thing; herds of walrus placidly hitch a ride in the spring on ice floes drifting with the north-flowing current. Walrus are found along both the Alaskan and Greenland Coasts, but the central Arctic has none.

Eskimo hunters paddled among the ice pans, often far from shore, looking for walrus herds. Even on days when thick fog had severely limited visibility, the herds could be located by their undulant belching and harrumphing — an unmistakable sound befitting an animal the size of a walrus.

An Eskimo woman makes a harpoon line from the stretched hide of a baby walrus. A hole is punched in the center of the hide and an unvarying width of line is cut in concentric circles with the *ulu* until the entire hide is used up.

Once the walrus herd was spotted sleeping on an ice floe, the hunters (most likely traveling in an umiak) would paddle over to another separate, small ice floe. After the boat was safely tied up they would chop several holes through the floe near the edge. The ends of their harpoon lines were secured to these. The small floe was then paddled closer to the herd. When within range all hunters would hurl their harpoons at a single, predesignated animal, which would roll off into the water as soon as hit. The walrus would soon tire of struggling against the ice floe and the hunters could paddle out to the animal to finish it off.

Walrus harpoons were the same shape as those used for whales, but smaller. These animals were harpooned from umiaks only when no convenient ice floes were present from which the task could be done. In such

A herd of walrus bask on an ice pan.

instances, inflated seal skin floats were attached to the end of the harpoon line and thrown overboard to create drag. The paddlers in the umiak would follow the floats until the walrus tired. It was not usually wise to allow a harpooned walrus to tow the umiak as it was sure to dive under an ice floe and demolish the umiak in tow. Stalks on foot were sometimes successful, but seldom were kayaks used as the walrus delighted in attacking these. Nor were the large umiaks immune to attacks by enraged walrus, and emergency repair supplies were always carried should the skin cover of the craft be punctured by a tusk. During an attack, if a walrus hooked his tusk over the gunnel of the boat, and this was not uncommon, the shear weight of the animal was certain to tip the boat over. Only whale hunting was treated with the same respect for inherent danger as was walrus hunting. The Eskimos understood well what an animal of the walrus' size and temperament could do. Even after a walrus had been killed and was being butchered, its comrades would linger a few yards away in the water — seemingly casting a vengeful eye toward the hunters.

In the eastern Arctic, Eskimos "fished" for walrus by dangling meat or blubber on a line. This bait was grabbed by the walrus and held between its foreflippers. Gradually, the reluctant walrus was pulled to the ice edge where it could be harpooned.

A wary approach is made to a herd of walrus on an ice floe. Hudson Bay region 1930

Pulling an animal such as a walrus — which might weigh as much as a ton (907 kilograms) — onto the ice for butchering required no small degree of mechanical skill. The most ingenious method was to chop three pairs of holes in a line on the ice a short distance back from the ice edge. The harpoon line was laced through these holes and in essence a block and tackle was formed to create a mechanical advantage that hoisted the huge body up onto the ice. In some circumstances, with a sloping ice foot, the carcass was butchered as it was pulled up out of the water. Once the walrus was secure on the ice, the chunk of flesh containing the buried harpoon tip was cut out of the animal so it could be replaced on the shaft. It was always important to wash all blood from the harpoon lines and out of the skin boats so it would not cause rotting.

State Historical Society of Wisconsin

A group of Hudson Bay region Eskimos go about the risky business of approaching a walrus herd from their umiak. **The harpooner is poised and ready in the bow of the boat.**

A large bull walrus has been pulled up on the ice edge in preparation for butchering — Alaskan Eskimo.

Whaling

The chase involved in whale hunting was a euphoric event. Success meant great social prestige to the crew of the strike boat and was immensely rewarding in products rendered for the entire village. Still, for all of this, it was a gravely dangerous undertaking. The hunting of these colossal mammals has been classically attributed to the Thule People. Petr Schledermann, director of the Arctic Institute of North America, has deduced from his excavations on Ellesmere Island that the importance of whale hunting may have been exaggerated. Though baleen and whale-bone are durable and reusable items, at one excavation site he found the total quantity of these products represented no more than 30 or 40 whales, even though that site had been occupied for about 700 years.

Sections of whale blubber backed by skin were called *muktuk* by the Inuit. Hazelnut flavored and high in calories, this food was rich in scurvy-preventing vitamin C. Surplus blubber was rendered into oil for the lamps. Whale ribs were used for house rafters, sled runners came from the jaw bone, and sinew was made from tendons of the flukes. Then there was baleen. Erroneously called whalebone, it was a very useful substance even in the world of white men before plastics were invented. The substance grew in comb-like sets of horny plates from the roof of the mouth in certain species of whales. The plates had a filamentous border that acted as an immense strainer while the whale swam through the water and sifted out tons of tiny crustaceans and pteropods, collectively called krill, from the rich Arctic seas. In such a manner, baleen provided whales with a very efficient filter-feeding mechanism. An important product of the white whaling fleets, this unique, tough and elastic substance was coveted for the manufacture of buggy whips, springs for the first typewriters and umbrella supports. Fashioned into staves, baleen buttressed ladies' corsets and made their hourglass figures possible. Eskimos were also ingenious, though considerably less vain, in adapting uses for this remarkable substance. They used it for harpoon lashings, vessels and containers, toboggans, fishing line, basket weaving in later times, snares, and a myriad of other items.

Whales came with the spring, swimming up through open leads in both the eastern and western Arctic. There were no whales in the central Arctic. But long before any leads opened, the Eskimos were anticipating their arrival by transporting umiaks out across perhaps several miles of land-fast ice to where the first permanent leads would form. The trail between this temporary whaling camp and the permanent camp of semi-subterranean houses on shore was improved to facilitate transportation by the women who chopped an easier path through the formidable piles of rafted ice. Then an expectant vigil began. With the umiaks positioned on the ice edge, their bows extending out over the water so they could be quickly and silently launched, the Inuit watched the waves for the telltale blows or surfacing black backs of a pod of whales. The surveillance

State Historical Society of Wisconsin

Piles of rafted ice makes a lofty perch for Eastern Canada Eskimos while watching for whales.

was a round-the-clock affair and done in shifts. Before retiring after a watch, the Eskimo would drink his fill of water so that a distended bladder would awaken him in a few hours and he could again take his turn at scanning the horizon. No chopping or knocking sounds could be made as it was felt (perhaps based more on superstition than fact) that this might alert the whales. In foggy weather the blowing was often heard before the whales could be seen. The Eskimos were even able to differentiate the short forceful puffs of the small white whales or belugas from the longer and deeper breathing of the large baleen whales such as the greys and bowheads.

The shafts of whaling harpoons were 8 or 9 feet (2 or 3 meters) in length. Being quite heavy and bulky, they were made for thrusting, not throwing. The timbers of wrecked ships were a bonanza to Eskimos for the purpose of manufacturing harpoon shafts. In pre-contact times it was difficult to find materials of the length or straightness necessary. In the eastern Arctic particularly, the tusk of the narwhal, that peculiar unicorn of the sea, was used for making whaling harpoons. The tip of the harpoon was designed to disengage from the shaft after being buried in the flesh of a whale. A harpoon line, made from the skin of the bearded seal or the walrus, was tied to the tip, or toggle, and had two or three sealskin floats tied to the other end. Each of these was able to furnish 200 to 300 pounds (91 to 136 kilograms) of drag.

The manner in which these seal skin floats were made deserves mention. The mouth of a seal carcass was enlarged by a cut through the throat. The entire body of the animal was then dexterously pulled through this opening as the skin was gradually everted. The hind flippers and tail were cut off and firmly tied together to form a neck for attaching the harpoon line. A wooden or ivory mouth piece with a stopper was tied into the head of the seal skin and it was through this that the skin was inflated. After laboring with such a project, reaching down inside the oily skin of a seal to pull out the flesh, the skinner was himself usually well greased from fingertips to armpits. Freshly voided urine with its high ammonia content was an admirable emulsifying agent and served best to wash the grease from the skinner.

Toggles were carved out of ivory and carried a single reverse barb to prevent them from being pulled out of the whale's flesh. The toggle contained a deep groove to hold a fragile, but razor-sharp, blade of slate or bone. The blade was held in place by a pin made from a short segment of tough walrus chin whisker or baleen. Extra blades were always carried and, in Alaska, lidded boxes carved from spruce in the shape of a whale were used to store these.

Once whales were spotted, the men hastily launched the boats and scrambled aboard. Deep, powerful strokes by the six paddlers soon had the umiak speeding toward a rendezvous with the whale. The entire crew of the boat consisted of eight men. The harpooner stood in the bow and shouted directions while the helmsman carried out part of the steering by manipulating a paddle-shaped rudder from the stern. The path to intercept the swimming whale was sometimes a tortuous one, twisting and turning through a maze of ice floes that were numerous at that time of year.

The umiak whaling crew functioned like a well-rehearsed team. Their respective roles were assumed by both tradition and training. Skills were learned through long apprenticeships with older whaling crews and honed to split-second perfection.

When traveling, whales would not dive to great depths, but instead swim just beneath the surface, rhythmically coming up for a breath of air every several seconds. This made it relatively easy to determine where the whale would surface next in his line of travel. As the sleek black wave of flesh of the whale's back rolled next to

A whaling crew has just made a strike. The harpooner prepares his weapon for the next strike while the crew member just behind him tosses the inflated sealskin floats that are attached to the harpoon line over board. The paddlers struggle to maneuver the *umiak* so they are not imperiled by the huge tail flukes.

the boat, the harpooner shouted for the crew to close the last few feet of distance that separated them. Twin spiracles atop the whale's head spouted condensation from the huge lungs as the harpooner braced himself and drove the harpoon with all his strength into the mammal. The toggle disengaged and the harpooner hung onto the shaft. The line slithered over the gunnel as the whale sounded. The

first paddler tossed the three inflated sealskin floats over the side while the harpooner fixed a second toggle with its own line and attached floats to the shaft. This line had been handily coiled to be ready when needed.

Immediately after the whale was struck, the crew's first responsibility was to draw paddle to make sure the huge tail flukes did not capsize the umiak when it came up behind the body. Then in the umiak they would follow the bubble trail left in the wake of the fleeing whale, the floats in tow. The whale would remain submerged for 4 or 5 minutes, and it was the floats popping to the surface that would alert the crew to when and where the whale was going to spout.

Chances of success were increased if two or more boats were used to close in on the quarry. A whale might have been struck 3 or 4 times and the drag from all the floats would add up to a ton or more. Such resistance would start exerting its effects and the whale would loll on the surface, gasping for air and would dive only when pushed. The harpooner had to decide when the whale was sufficiently exhausted to be warily re-approached for the killing lance to be used. Unlike the harpoon tip which was designed to pierce the whale's skin and affix itself, the lance had a long, slender, non-detachable point for penetration through the thick layer of blubber and into a vital organ.

The well-developed sensory apparatus of the whale let it know where its tormentors were and when they were approaching, but the drag produced by the many floats would become too much. The hunters would relentlessly pursue the beleaguered animal and its exhaustion would prevent it from making a prolonged run away from the umiak when the crew approached with the killing lance. The dives became shorter and in between them multiple jabs were made with the lance until at last the whale would not be able to dive beneath the surface. Now the smaller geysers of spray from the dying whale's respiration were

tained crimson red from blood in the lungs. The tangled
arpoon lines formed a mosaic over the body of the whale
s life ebbed and it floated motionless on the water.

Not infrequently the chase ended a long distance from
here it had begun. The whaling crew wasted no time in
ttaching lines to the shaft of the tail so the slain animal
ould be towed to camp. Small carved, ivory hooks about
ve inches (13 centimeters) long were made in pairs and
ttached to each other by a short, stout thong. One of
ese was pushed through a double slit made in the whale's
kin under the flipper and the other through a hole in the
ipper itself. This served to hold the flippers close to the
ody so they would not hinder towing the whale.

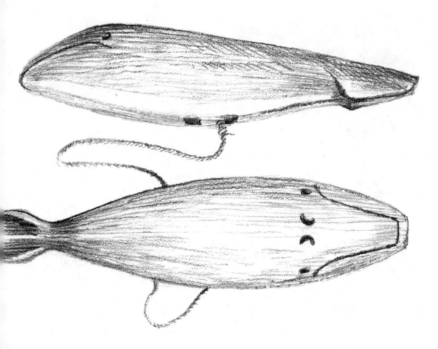

ory flipper toggles such as these are used to secure the fins of the
aughtered whale close to its body. In this manner the fins do not
eate drag while the whale is being towed to shore.

Bowhead whales were huge: up to 60 feet (18 meters) in length and weighing perhaps 60 tons (54,000 kilograms). Grey whales were only slightly smaller. A single large bowhead might produce 30 tons (27,000 kilograms) of blubber and have 800 baleen plates that were 12 or 13 feet (3.7 or 4 meters) long.

The butchering of such an animal was an onerous task that would take an entire village a full day or more. If the whaling camp were on the edge of land-fast ice, some distance from the permanent camp, much time and effort had to be expended to drag the slabs of blubber back. The ground in camp would literally be covered with the checker-board pattern of squares of blubber.

Strips of whale meat drying on racks near Hooper Bay

Alaskan Eskimos prepare to butcher a beluga.

Belugas are a smaller species of whale that were hunted by the Eskimos. Creamy white in color and inhabiting arctic waters, these most skittish of whales seldom exceed 18 feet (5 meters) in length and a weight of 3,500 pounds (1,588 kilograms). Belugas are members of the order of toothed whales, called *Odontoceti*, as opposed to the *Mysticeti* order — the baleen whales. These white whales were called "sea canaries" by the early sailors because of the multitude of audible sounds they made. Descriptions of their chatter have been as diverse as their apparent repertoire. They have been said to chortle, click, chirp, groan, squeak, and trill.

The beluga's extremely nervous disposition made it

impossible to approach from a boat unless it was cornered in a bay and driven up into the shallows where it would become stranded and could be harpooned. In the fall, babiche nets, similar to those used for seals, were set around reefs for belugas. Heavy anchor stones were used to hold the nets down but still, if an entire pod of belugas hit the net, they would carry it with them and it would be lost. Late in the fall belugas would occasionally linger too long in a coastal inlet and their exit would become blocked by ice. Such occurrences, rare as they were, furnished the Eskimos with an easy harvest.

Being toothed whales, belugas fed on salmon and char. These whales could sometimes be seen herding their prey with the tide into small inlets. Under conditions such as these, the timorous belugas could have their excitable nature turned against them. A few saplings were cut and stuck in the bottom across the isthmus of the cove. The ebbing tide rushing past these vibrating stakes would create an unfamiliar sound barrier which the belugas refused to pass, and they would warily retreat back to the top of the inlet. As the tide dropped further, they would become stranded, and the waiting Inuit would only need to come in with their knives and ropes.

Polar Bear Hunting

It is not without reason that the polar bear is classified as a marine mammal. Seldom does this great bear go on land, even to give birth. Like the Eskimo, the only other predator to hunt on the polar ice pack, the polar bear's existence is tied to the seal. The Inuit called him *nanook* which means "the ever wandering one" or "the lonely roamer" because he shuns the protected inlets and sounds in lieu of areas of greater ice movement. It is here that leads are opening and seals may be found in open water. Such conditions are not essential for the polar bear's success for the animal is also adept at its own style of breathing hole hunting. Lying in wait next to the hole, the bear will pounce on the vent when the seal appears rapidly clawing away the ice covering and pinning the seal.

A polar bear cannot outrun a pack of sled dogs for long. Here *nanook* is held at bay while the Eskimo hunter approaches with his spear.

Polar bears were not hunted perhaps as much as they were encountered. Still, when Knud Rasmussen once asked an elderly Eskimo what he considered the greatest happiness in his life, he replied, "to run across fresh bear tracks and be ahead of all other sledges."

Polar bear tracks contained a fine ridge of snow that formed between the creases of the toes. If this ripple of raised snow was firm, the tracks were old. On the other hand, soft snow within the tracks meant the bear could not be far ahead and the trail was worth following. The presence of ravens, those ubiquitous scavengers, flying out over the ice suggested that the remains of a recent seal kill were present and alerted hunters that a bear might be near.

Sled dogs seem to have an inborn hatred of polar bears. Whenever a canine caught wind of one, it eagerly took chase. So enthusiastic was it about this that if the Eskimo didn't have a firm grip on the upstanders of his sled and fell off, he could never hope to overtake the team. When the hunter had the opportunity, he released his lead dog to pursue the bear and followed with the team. The Norwegian physiologist, Dr. Nils Oritsland, has noted that the excellent insulation provided by the polar bear's fur and fat layer makes heat dissipation very difficult. They will overheat when forced to run a long distance and can be quickly brought to bay by dogs. When the bear stopped running in order to make his stand, the remainder of the dogs were released from the sled to surround the animal. The Inuit now had only to pick his way through the bawling dogs, hopefully not attracting too much attention to himself, and use his spear.

Certainly the polar bear was the Eskimo's greatest land-dwelling adversary, but the risk of the hunt was compensated for by the products derived from a bear kill. Most important of these was the hide, which made superb winter trousers. The average polar bear hide had sufficient material for three pairs. As was usually the case, several hunters were responsible for subduing the animal and they would divide the skin among themselves. The hunter who rushed in and struck the bear first got the most desirable piece of hide, which was the upper part with forelegs. This section contained the long guard hairs of the ruff and made the warmest trousers. The first hunter would measure from the neck down with his whip handle marking the length he required, and then cut his part off. The second hunter did likewise, and the next until the hide was used up.

The meat was eaten but it was of far less value than the treasured polar bear hide. Flesh from polar bears was always heavily infested with trichinosis and could never be eaten raw. The liver was toxic even to dogs and had to be carefully discarded. Being the richest naturally occurring concentration of Vitamin A, it caused a severe medical condition known as hypervitaminosis A when consumed.

Caribou Hunting

Marine mammals have an affinity for the ice edge. Whales, walruses, seals, and the polar bears that stalk them all ply this water/ice breakpoint for their livelihoods. These waters, thriving with wildlife, produced well for the Inuit hunter in the winter and spring. But as the warmer days of summer melted the landfast ice, and as north-bound currents carried away the main pack with its attendant ice floes, the plentitude of game moved with it. The open sea that was left became relatively devoid of life. The Eskimos then had to turn their attention landward to the caribou, which they called *tuktu*.

The main caribou kill took place in the fall when the animals were gathering into herds for their migration. In the summer, when caribou were widely dispersed and grazing across the tundra, various stalking techniques worked best. Seldom were the animals sufficiently grouped at this time for a successful mass kill. Still, the harvest of these summer animals was important because their hair was short and it was these hides that were most ideal for fashioning into winter garments.

Sometimes a head-on approach with bows and arrows held upright over the head to simulate antlers was successful on the shortsighted caribou. At other times a complete reversal of this tactic whetted the animals' curiosity and they might follow two men walking directly away from them. When a stone cairn or depression in the ground was reached, one of the hunters would drop off while his companion continued. The caribou was then shot as it walked by the concealed hunter.

Two hunters working as a team were also able to profit from the caribou's tendency to double around when spooked from a certain spot and then return to that original area. The two hunters, walking close together so as to appear as one, would approach a small band of grazing caribou until they took flight. One hunter would then immediately conceal himself close to the ground while the other continued to pressure the animals. The caribou would flee in a wide semi-circular pattern and return close to where the first hunter was hiding, who would then likely be afforded a close shot. This would in turn frighten the caribou toward the second hunter who was by now concealed, and in this manner they could continue volleying the bewildered animals back and forth between them.

Young boys had great sport running down and physically overpowering calves. Cows with young calves were especially wary of wolves and the boys howling like wolves were able to drive the wild-eyed caribou into an ambush of hunters waiting in shallow excavated pits.

As the herds began to form toward the end of summer and travel routes became more defined, rawhide nooses set between stakes or strong bushes were effective. The noose would be held open by strands of grass tied to the loop and an adjacent bush or stake. Pitfalls, some con-

An Eskimo hunter near the present town of Wainwright, Alaska has brought a large bull caribou back to camp on his sled.

taining an impaling spike in the bottom, were used only rarely. Just as with the Athapaskans, river and lake crossings offered some of the best opportunities for a large kill. The kayaks used on inland waters for this type of hunting, particularly in the central Arctic, were smaller and more fragile than their counterparts used on the open seas of Alaska and Greenland. They were also considerably lighter and more transportable.

93

Caribou meat was boiled fresh and air-dried into jerky. Children coveted the raw eyes, and the lichens and vegetable matter contained within the stomach and fermented by the gastric juices were relished by all. Strips of back fat were cut into small pieces and chewed by the women until well mixed with saliva and converted to a pasty consistency and then spat into a bowl. When an ample amount had been prepared, some pieces of fish, water and perhaps berries were added and all were stirred into a homogeneous mass. This concoction was considered a delicacy and was served at feasts and to guests.

The hide with its superb insulating qualities was the most durable product of the caribou. It could be prepared with the hair left on or with the hair off by two separate processes. In both instances, the flesh side was well scraped to remove all clinging particles of meat. If the hair was to be removed, the skin was then rolled into a bundle with the hair side inward and stored inside where it could ripen in the warmth. This allowed the hair to slip. Sometimes this process was facilitated by dipping the hide into hot water. The hair was then scraped off. Babiche was laced through slits around the periphery of the hide and it was allowed to dry and stretch on a frame or on the ground if no driftwood was available. When this cardboard-stiff hide was needed for use, it was softened by pulling it back and forth across a scraper held firmly upright or abraded with a piece of pumice stone. The final softening was attained through meticulous chewing by the women.

When the hair was to be left on the hide, the flesh side was covered with urine which was collected in a communal bowl in the igloo. It was then rolled into a compact bundle with the hair side out and kept in the warm confines of the dwelling for a day or so. Next it was unrolled, and after all remaining fragments of flesh had been removed, was hung over a smouldering lamp until dry and thoroughly preserved by the smoke. Still quite brittle, the hide had to be scraped to break the grain and to render it pliable. Fish roe or decayed brains were then worked into the flesh side for their oiling effect to preserve the softness. A final scraping and a kneading of the skin between the hands produced a beautifully tanned hide that had a satiny white quality on the inside with the hair and its insulating qualities remaining on the outside.

Other Hunting Methods

Musk oxen were only occasionally hunted by the Inuit. Sections of their horns were spliced into bows and the heavy wool of the hide, called *qiviut*, was also used. Dogs were used to bring the oxen to bay in the same manner as polar bears. Their technique for hunting musk oxen varied little from that of the subarctic Athapaskans.

Arctic wolves were killed for their fur, used primarily to line parkas. The wolf was an extremely cunning animal — usually too smart to be foiled by box traps or dead falls. Only the most clever of devices — and some were hideously cruel — were successful in taking wolves.

Popularized in many tales of the Arctic are "wolf pills." These were made from strips of baleen pointed on each end and folded spring fashion into a helical configuration. To prevent the natural elasticity of the strips of baleen from straightening themselves back out, they were tied in their coiled position with a piece of sinew. The sinew binding was cut after the "pill" had been frozen solid. This parcel was then buried in a piece of blubber and left where an unsuspecting wolf was certain to gobble it down. As this contrivance rapidly thawed in the wolf's stomach, the coiled baleen strip sprang back to its original shape. The

A herd of musk ox strike their classic defense pose.

pointed ends would pierce the stomach of the wolf and perhaps other vital organs as well. The resulting internal hemmorrhage was a trap no wolf could escape. The Inuit hunter had only to follow the ravens to claim his kill. It is possible that larger versions of these were also used on polar bears.

Another method that operated on this same principle was made from a sharp bone knife. The splintered lower leg bone of a caribou was ideal. These were smeared with blood and fat and then buried in the snow with only the sharp edge protruding. Wolves would be attracted and ravenously lick the knife edge. In doing so they would lacerate their tongues. The taste of their own fresh blood only goaded them on further until the large arteries at the base of the tongue were severed. The bleeding was profuse and they would soon die.

The arctic fox, a drab brown coloration in the summer, becomes ermine-white in the winter. They are small animals with little meat and fragile hides. Fox tails were used as mops or sponges about the igloo or boat to soak up blood or other messes that were left after butchering game. When they became thoroughly saturated, they were tossed into a simmering pot to render flavor to the broth. On the whole, little effort was expended in catching foxes until the advent of the white fur trade when considerable commercial value was attached to the winter pelts.

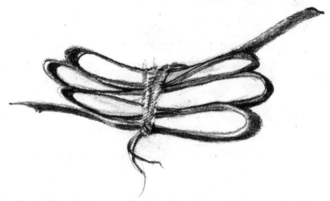

Deadly "wolf pills" are made from sharpened slivers of baleen, folded into a helical configuration and frozen into position.

Foxes were scavengers and in the winter roamed the pack ice in search of a polar bear's old kill so they might finish the scant remains. The polar bear is a somewhat finnicky eater, eating only the skin and blubber of seals and leaving the rest. With their sensitive noses, the Arctic fox could detect a meal buried under several feet of snow and ice. Yellow snow from the Arctic foxes' urine helped Eskimos locate their fall caribou caches, and similar claim markers of polar bear seal kills spelled the difference between life and death for more than a few hunters stranded on ice floes. Life was easier for the Arctic fox in the summer because gleanings were abundant around bird cliffs which they frequented, and also prowling the beaches they could find carrion tossed up by the sea.

Since Arctic foxes were relatively easily baited, they were particularly susceptible to tower traps.

The carrion-eating habits of the Arctic fox made them easy to bait, and being less wary then the wolf, they were susceptible to box-type enclosure traps and to deadfalls using heavy driftwood logs or rocks. The simplest enclosure trap was a miniature stone hut with a trapdoor. This was baited with seal meat and after the fox had entered and started eating, the hunter, who was hidden nearby, would pull a cord that tripped the trapdoor. Pitfalls were effective and often had sharp antler spikes in the bottom to impale the fox and prevent it from leaping back out. Strips of whale baleen were stuck into the lip of the pit and allowed to protrude over the opening to form a covering. A snow covering was sprinkled over these to camouflage the trap, but the elasticity of the baleen would permit the fox to fall into the pit.

Tower traps were constructed from piled stones or ice blocks and baited with seal entrails. At first the bait would be made easily obtainable by leaving a few stones or blocks out of the base of the tower. Only after the foxes had become accustomed to feeding at the trap would the portal be closed and a ramp leading to the top installed. The tower traps were of sufficient height that once the fox had entered via this route, it was impossible to jump back out.

The tension trap was an ingenious device that was commonly used to catch foxes along the Alaskan coast. A cylinder of wood contained twisted sinew cords that furnished spring for a lever. The lever contained a sharp ivory or bone spicule that "brained" the fox when it attempted to steal the bait, pulling the trigger which released the lever.

Arctic hares round out the mammal harvest of the Eskimo. Snares made either of sinew or thin strips of baleen were set in the runways among bushes. Rabbits were also driven into fine sinew nets that were set at the openings in the underbrush.

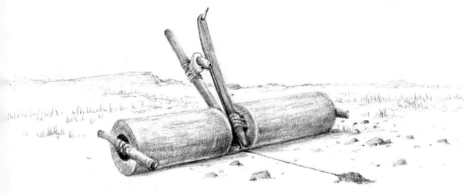

Tension traps were used for arctic foxes along the Alaskan coast.

Bird Hunting

Eskimos depended almost entirely on hunting for subsistence and gathering played a very minor role in their acquisition of food. Still, in certain parts of the Arctic, visiting the bird cliffs to gather eggs was a rite of summer. Auks by the millions nested along those portions of the Arctic coasts that had tall cliffs with ledges and crevices. Nets were rolled into a long cylinder and lashed tightly. This served as a cable that was lowered over the edge of the cliff. The mesh afforded good finger and toe holds for the climber who descended the face of the cliff and filled a babiche bag slung over his shoulder with delicious eggs.

The parent birds, too, were caught right off their nests with a bag net on a handle. Somewhat more effective was a net of fine sinew suspended between two long poles and placed close to the cliffs.

These auks became the main ingredient of a feast dish when they were stuffed in their entirety — feathers, feet, beak and all — into a freshly skinned sealskin bag with copious amounts of blubber still sticking to the flesh side. These sealskin bags were flensed from the carcass in the same manner as the skins that were removed to be made into floats. Once the bag was filled with birds, it was tied shut and cached away. The blubber became liquified as decay progressed and seeped into the fermenting raw birds. Several months later the putrifying mass was opened and gleefully consumed.

Gulls, terns and some species of waterfowl nested on small offshore islands or rocks to avoid land predators. These "egg islands" were visited by the Inuit not only to collect the eggs but also to set sinew and baleen slip-nooses around the nests to catch the adults when they returned.

During summer months, eggs were gathered from the bird cliffs.

In the winter, flat snow houses with a thin sheet of translucent ice set as a window pane in the roof were constructed. A hunter, lying inside, could see a gull when it lit to take a piece of bait that had been left on the roof, and could immediately break through the snow and ice roof and grab the gull by the feet. Bone gorges baited with a piece of meat and tied by a length of sinew to a stake were also effective in catching gulls. In addition to the flesh which was eaten, tendons from the wings of gulls were prized for the manufacture of fine but strong fishing line.

Arctic loons could be attracted by imitating their calls, and were shot with a bow and stunning arrow. The webbed feet of these birds were split and made into small "possible" bags and their moisture-proof skin made a good seat for wet surfaces.

The winds from the south that accompany spring in the Arctic bring flocks of waterfowl and shorebirds in nearly endless succession. Snow geese, black brant, white-fronted geese, pintails, old squaws, Stellar's eiders, common eiders, king eiders, spectacled eiders and red-breasted mergansers all ride a tail wind to return to their ancestral nesting grounds. Hunters of all ages carried *bolas* (their lengths shortened by a series of slip knots for convenience) about their necks to capitalize on this migrating abundance. When low-flying ducks or geese were spotted, these bolas were swung around the head to pick up momentum and then released. Once in the air these strange but effective weapons would open up like a giant flying spider and wrap around the neck, body, wings and feet of the bird which would in turn come tumbling to the ground totally incapacitated. These bolas were usually made of sinew with beluga teeth or sections of caribou antler for weights. A small wooden tab served as a tie for the lines and as a pinch-hold while twirling the weapon.

Ducks, unlike migrating geese, skimmed low over the sea, just clearing the crests of waves. These could be caught with sinew nets fastened between poles or ice piles over parts of the sea that were still frozen. Just as a flock approached, the net would be quickly raised. As the ducks plummeted into the net, they either became entangled or fell to the ice where they were pounced upon before they could fly away.

An Eskimo bird spear.

Bolas were routinely carried by hunters, draped about their necks, during the waterfowl migration season.

103

When a very dense fog was accompanied by cold temperatures during waterfowl migration, the feathers of ducks became laden with frozen condensation. This extra weight greatly increased the labor of their flight. Under such conditions, Eskimos would go out to the line of flight and, concealed by the fog, wait for the flocks to approach. Forewarned by their calling, the hunters would wait quietly until the ducks were almost upon them, and then, just at the critical moment, jump up and shout. The startled ducks, attempting to bank sharply, would spin out of control due to their iced feathers and crash to the ground where they were caught by hand.

Once the migrating flocks had divided up into mating pairs and serious nesting was underway, baleen nooses attached to long lines were successfully employed. These were set along the shores and even across the water near nesting areas. For the diving fish-eating species of ducks, the traps were most effective when set just beneath the surface of the water. Later in the summer when the adults were in their eclipse plummage, they were stalked in kayaks and shot with stunning arrows or killed with bird spears. The latter had, in addition to a point on the tip, three ivory points angled out from the mid part of the shaft to increase the target radius and make a hit more likely.

The docile ptarmigan could be killed by accurately throwing rocks and, while never a major item on the menu, did offer some variety. These year-round residents survive the winter by eating buds and twigs from centuries-old dwarf Arctic willow trees that grow gnarled and twisted close to the ground in the valleys. The bird's crop containing this partially digested mass was an especially savory tidbit for the hunter.

Sinew and baleen snares were set amongst bushes where ptarmigan fed and roosted in the winter. Sometimes, specially constructed brush fences led meandering ptarmigan to openings where nooses were set. During the spring mating season, the ptarmigan's courtship displays and marking of territory rituals were used in decoying. A ptarmigan skin, crudely stuffed with grass was placed on a prominent knoll. Sinew netting was strung around the imposter, and with the aid of ptarmigan territorial calls made by the hidden hunter, the male ptarmigan soon came to the defense of his domain. After the Eskimo claimed his chivalrous but entangled victim, he would roll up his net and take his stuffed decoy to the vicinity of another male ptarmigan.

Smithsonian Institution — Photo by E.W. Nelson 1877-1881

An Unaligmiut Alaskan Eskimo casts a bird spear from his kayak during the summer waterfowl moulting season.

Fishing

Even among the Eskimos, perhaps the greatest hunters of mammals of all native peoples, fishing still served as a vital link. Caches of dried arctic char were essential to Eskimo survival in the fall until sea ice became suitable for breathing-hole hunting. This was especially true if the caribou harvest was a poor one. But the char catch was usually predictable, and their richness as a food source was manifested by the oil that dripped freely from their blood-red flesh on warm days as they dried on the racks. Driftwood was too precious to burn for the smoking of fish: it was more wisely used in the manufacture of sleds, kayak frames and other essentials. The char were split and hung on racks to dry in the sun.

National Museum of Canada, Ottawa

An Eskimo fisherman sits beside his caribou-skin tent while fish dry on racks in the background.

The Arctic char is a salmonid fish that is anadromous in its habits. They spend the summer in salt water, not far from the mouths of rivers which they will ascend in the fall. In these freshwater rivers they will spawn and spend the winter — returning to saltwater the following spring. Tent camps of the Eskimos were moved to the shores of arctic rivers during the char run specifically along a shallow stretch. Here two stone dams were built. The lower one had a small opening through which the char could pass, but the upper dam completely blocked their migration. The pool between these stone weirs served as a holding pen where the milling fish were speared with fish leisters. These leisters had center prongs of ivory and flanking barbs of baleen or musk ox horn.

National Museum of Canada, Ottawa
Eskimo spearing char with their leisters at the stone weir.

The skin tents were positioned close to the river so a sharp eye could be kept for fish entering the holding basin. When a school of char had passed through the lower weir, the men quickly took off their trousers and tied their sealskin boots around their legs just below the knee. In no way did this keep water out of their boots, but the water that did enter was somewhat trapped and gradually became warmed by their legs — a relative improvement over the frigid water of the river. The entrance to the lower weir was sealed shut with rocks so the char could not escape. Each Inuit carried in his mouth a long bone needle attached to a sealskin thong. As the fish were speared and pulled from the leister, they were skewered through the gills with the bone needle and put onto the stringer.

Before the women with their ulus could get to the strings of fish pulled up on shore to split them for drying, the children were eagerly digging out the eyes to eat. The adults preferred the heads of fish which had been buried and allowed to decay. These were dug up and pulverized into an evil-smelling paste and eaten. Much of the dried fish was stored in caches that could be returned to throughout the winter to supplement the Eskimos' seal diet. The caches were constructed of river gravel spread on the ground and ringed with large boulders. The dried char were then placed within this stone enclosure and covered with large flat stones to discourage raiding by animal scavengers.

An Eskimo man, carrying a fish stringer in his mouth, spears char with a leister within the confines of a stone weir.

National Museum of Canada, Ottawa

Alaskan Eskimo jigging for tom cod through the ice.

Whitefish and tom cod were fished for through the ice. Meshed gill nets made of baleen or sinew were set under the ice for whitefish in the same fashion as sealing nets. Tom cod, on the other hand, were jigged for by using a short pole, line, and a lure. The fishing line was made from thin strips of baleen joined by a special knot. Apparently baleen offered special advantages as a material for lines under such cold conditions. It had a natural elasticity that prevented it from kinking, and ice, which would not readily adhere to it, could be shaken off. The barbed lures were carved from ivory and embellished with bits of bright red beaks from puffins to make them more attractive to the cod.

An ivory tom cod jig. The leader is made from a loop of baleen tied together with sinew.

109

Hummocks of ice extended below the level of the surface ice and it was in the lee of such breaks that tom cod preferred to congregate. Just as the direction of the current shifts, so would tom cod move their position in relation to the hummock. The first hole that an Eskimo cut in the ice near a hummock may have been solely to test the direction of the current. A small chunk of ice was forced beneath the hole to see in which direction it drifted off. If the direction indicated that the hole was in the lee of the ice hummock, that is where the Eskimo fished. Otherwise, he moved to the appropriate side.

When jigging for tom cod an ice scoop was held in one hand to constantly rid the hole of forming ice crystals. When a fish was felt nosing the lure, the Eskimo gave the line a quick jerk to hook it. A bight of line was then caught with the ice scoop in one hand and drawn over to be caught on a peg of the jigging stick. This was in turn drawn over toward the ice scoop so that the line was drawn up in long hanks alternately between these two sticks. In this manner, the line was retrieved without being touched. After the tom cod was brought to the surface, a dexterous jerk unhooked the fish and it fell to the ice to freeze almost instantly. The jig was quickly lowered back down the hole before the school moved on. The cod that had been caught were placed in a circle around the fisherman with their heads pointing toward the hole. Such a practice was thought to assure the Inuit that he would continue to be amidst a school of fish.

In this northern world of snow and ice, man's creativity, fortitude and courage were taxed to the extreme. The howling wind, the creaking ice, the whimpering dogs, and even the cold were the Eskimo's welcome companions for most of the year. Only starvation was the occasional visitor they did not wish to greet. The rigors of the Eskimos' environment seemed to intensify not only their indomitable will to survive in this hostile land, but also their drive to live life to the fullest measure.

An Eskimo woman jigging for tom cod uses her ice scoop and jigging stick to retrieve line.

Grizzly bear Larry Halverson

Hunters of the Northern Forest

The Canadian North Woods is a land rife with the great legends of voyageurs and their indomitable bourgeois, of trappers, legendary hunters, fur traders and of famous explorers. Once a person has been to the boreal forests, he will never forget it. The mystique and beauty, the wildness, call one back and a north woodsman is born forever.

The North Woods seems like an infinity of trees and water. It is the farthest north of three great forest belts that girdle the North American land mass.

The mark of distinction of the North Woods is the conifer; pine and spruce dominate the scene. But, it is not a homogeneous forest. The ghostly white trunks of birch trees shimmer through the towering white spruce and the slightest wind rustles the leaves of aspens. It is a riverine environment and the edges of lakes and sloughs and the sandbars along rivers are blanketed with willows and alders, giving much of the country a very brushy character. At intervals the heavy forest opens up into swampy, grassy meadows. In these low-lying areas, black spruce, stunted and scrawny when compared to white spruce, are far more tolerant of the moisture. It is the birch however that has most affected the economy of the Indians of the subarctic boreal forests. From its paper-like bark, these people fashioned their canoes and all sorts of boxes, containers and vessels.

As one travels north, it becomes apparent that the North Woods starts losing its battle to the climate. The birch are the first to go, then the great white spruce. Only the black spruce, stunted and misshapen, growing aslant with branches only on their leeward side, make their last

114

The woodland and barren ground caribou were a
main staple of the hunters of the northern forest.

Bear and wolves shared man's desire for game. Here a moose, probably a winter kill, has been scavenged by a black bear.

stand against the cold and the savage winds. The Great North Woods has been scourged into "the land of little sticks".

This far north land above the boreal forests is the tundra. The very mention of this word evokes visions of ultimate desolation. Apparently featureless at first, of an interminable sameness, this land offers one the extreme loneliness of being adrift on a terrestial sea. Only the wave-like pattern of glacier-flattened hills and the network of lakes and rivers breaks the monotony. Tundra forms its own ecosystem, covering limitless miles of land like a plush, resilient carpet of mosses, lichens, sedges, grasses and stunted bushes. Napped with a multitude of diminutive flowers that present a colorful panorama during the short subarctic summer, tundra invites scrutiny at hand and knee level. Even the dull gray-granite boulders strewn across the landscape add their splash of color to the scene with kaleidoscopic mosaics of brilliant lichens clinging to their surfaces. These lichens are actually composed of alga and fungus in a symbiotic relationship, and are extremely hardy so as to withstand the rigors of this climate. A specimen only an inch (2.5 centimeters) in diameter may be two thousand years old. Lichens are perhaps the most ancient living things on earth.

The line of demarcation between tundra and the boreal forests is not precise. They meld into each other. To the east, that great inland sea, the Hudson Bay, pushes the treeline far to the south, well below the 60th parallel. Just as pockets of tundra exist among the black and white spruce and the birch, so, too, there are oases of trees well up in the arctic tundra. The valley of the Thelon River, for example, located far inside tundra country, is tree-lined along its entire course until it empties into Chesterfield Inlet and, from there, into Hudson Bay.

The vastness of the western reaches of the subarctic land is regularly punctuated by mountains and river valleys

— more so than the east. Two mighty river systems, the Yukon and the Mackenzie, traverse the interior of Alaska and the Yukon Territory and have sculpted the landscape over eons of time. Whereas eastern portions of tundra had their mountains compressed by glacier movement, this sea of ice did not extend into the Yukon Valley or the interior of Alaska to exert its awesome leveling effect on the terrain there.

Cold is the real curse of the North Country. In winter the frozen surfaces of lakes and rivers are covered with blowing snow and become indistinguishable from the surrounding land. Temperatures plummet to -70 degrees Fahrenheit (-57° Celsius) and the tundra and boreal forests are transformed into a white hell.

During the brief respite of the subarctic summer, temperatures can soar to over 100 degrees Fahrenheit (38° Celsius). Now there are other tormentors to challenge the sanity of any man who invades the tundra or boreal forests. Hordes of blood-sucking insects, mosquitoes and black flies, immediately attack any patch of exposed skin to extract nourishment. Even their incessant droning as they hover about one's body is enough to make a man claw his way to the highest ridge for a breath of air.

Even on the warmest summer days a bit of winter still lurks just below the ground in tundra country. This entire land has been underlaid since the ice age with a permanently frozen stratum of earth and ice called permafrost. The insulation of the tundra-covering keeps it from melting and provides a handy icebox for the arctic dweller. Rainfall is scant on both the tundra and the boreal forests. The tundra in particular is so dry that on the basis of annual precipitation alone, the area would be classified as a desert. Still vegetation is able to thrive because the permafrost prevents water from the ice and snow that melt in the spring from running off or sinking deep down.

Caribou are the most common big-game animals in the

The grey-brown stone sheep (here) and its white cousin, the Dall sheep, share the high country, the fisher (here), or its smaller relative the marten share the forest, and the beaver (here) and muskrat share the waterways with the northern hunters.

Deerskin being soaked by Carrier Indians.

Moulting flocks of waterfowl are flightless for several weeks and readily harvested.

The spruce grouse is distributed across the entire boreal forest and was easy prey when encountered.

subarctic. There are three different species inhabiting various areas and they live primarily on caribou moss which is not really a moss but a lichen (*caladonia*). Moose are prevalent, as well as both black and grizzly bears. The grizzly is the only bear species that inhabits the far north tundra areas. The musk ox, a curious beast, is well-equipped to inhabit the most inhospitable, farthest north regions. Snowshoe hares, porcupines, ground squirrels and red fox are common or rare depending on relatively predictable natural cyclic fluctuations. Wolves and muskrats were important mammals to prehistoric people in the subarctic while furbearers, such as beaver, mink, and lynx, had their major impact on native economy after white contact had initiated the fur trade.

The north country is this continent's major waterfowl nesting area and species that are seasonally present include mallards, pintails, green-winged teal, American widgeon, common goldeneyes, buffleheads, greater scaup, white-winged scoters, red-breasted mergansers, common loons, arctic loons, and Canada, snow, and white-fronted geese. Willow ptarmigan, who have become masters at camouflage by molting and growing new plummage seasonally to match their background, are common in the valleys. Three species of grouse, spruce, ruffed, and sharp-tailed, are represented in various areas of the subarctic. Ravens, gray jays, sandhill cranes, snowy owls and jaegers are all birds residing in the north.

Rivers and lakes that have sufficient depth to support life, boast impressive concentrations of whitefish, inconnu (shee fish), grayling, burbot, pike, suckers, and trout.

Hudson Bay roughly divides the subarctic region into two separate ethnographic categories: the Athapaskan culture to the west and the Algonquin to the east. While the division is based on linguistics, it also reflects a different prehistory for the two groups. The Algonquins were dwellers of the sparsely-treed southern fringes of the interior and the heavily forested portions of eastern Canada. They originally came from the south and are descendants of the Eastern Woodland Indians whose culture theirs resemble almost indistinguishably. The largest tribe is the Cree who live south and southwest of Hudson Bay. The most westerly Cree inhabit the prairie provinces of Canada. Their lifestyle shows a strong Plains Indian influence and they are referred to as the Plains Cree. The Montagnais and the Naskapi Tribes live east of Hudson Bay in the wooded portions of Quebec and on the Labrador Peninsula.

The immense area west of Hudson Bay and into the interior of Alaska is the home of the numerous tribes of the Athapaskan linguistic stock. Inhabitation of such a vast geographical area has led to large numbers of locally adapted survival techniques designed to sustain life in such a harsh environment. Many of these skills were borrowed by Athapaskans from neighboring cultures such as the Eskimo to the north, or Northwest Coast people to the west. The Athapaskan language has perhaps exhibited a greater stability than many other aspects of their early culture. Even though there are many regional dialects, the most far-flung groups are still usually able to communicate with each other.

The word Athapaskan is actually a Cree (Algonquin) term meaning "strangers of the north", and refers to a single tribe that lived near Canada's Lake Athabaska. This designation became all-inclusive only in the post-contact era. The Athapaskans called themselves *Dene*. This meant literally, "the people," as do most self-appointed descriptions of primitive men, and gives insight into the all-encompassing view they held of themselves in relation to their world.

The Athapaskan tribes of the Canadian interior are the Chipewyan (not to be confused with the Ojibwa-Chippewa of the Lake Superior region) west of Hudson

Bay; the Beaver along the lower Peace River in Northern Alberta; the Slave along the southern shore of Great Slave Lake; the Dogrib between Great Slave Lake and Great Bear Lake; the Hare northwest of Great Bear Lake; the Kaska or Nahani west of the headwaters of the Mackenzie River; the Sekani in central British Columbia; the Carrier (named from their custom of forcing widows to carry the charred bones of their dead husbands on their backs) in southwestern British Columbia; the Chilcotin south of the Carrier's lands; the Tahltan on the upper Stikine River in northwestern British Columbia; and the Tutchone in southern Yukon Territory.

Tribes of the Alaska interior are the Han on the Alaska-Yukon border; the Kutchin or Loucheux occupying the Yukon River Valley and the land east to the Mackenzie; the Tanaina around Cook Inlet; the Ingalik along the lower Yukon River and the Koyukon west of the confluence of the Yukon and Porcupine Rivers. This was the general distribution of Athapaskan tribes at the time of the first white contact, and is thought to roughly parallel tribal areas of the preceding 1000-2000 years although some regional shifts have occurred.

The skin tents, bone tools and other perishable possessions of the Athapaskans have given archaeologists few clues to their pre-history. One fact is certain; we are dealing with relatively recent inhabitation within the total time span of man in North America. The land itself is new, — only about 8000 years ago did it emerge from beneath the mile-thick (11.6 kilometer-thick) glaciers of the Pleistocene Era.

The first inhabitants of the Barrens may have moved into the area from the plains shortly after the retreat of the glacier. Their stone points and lifestyle differed little from archaic cultures existing to the south at the time. Meanwhile the upper Yukon Territory became peopled with fresh newcomers from Siberia. (They may have existed for a time in Central Alaska.) Theirs was a distinct culture characterized by long, flat flints with parallel-sided flakes capable of taking on an amazingly sharp edge. These were adapted to use in a number of implements. These people are now referred to as the Microblade Culture.

The Plains migrants who were living in the central subarctic were replaced by a proto-Eskimo people who crossed Bering Strait about 6000 years ago. These newcomers may have migrated along the arctic coasts and drifted south seeking a warmer climate, or possibly they struck out directly across the interior of Alaska and Canada until they reached Hudson Bay. This was a very short occupation, perhaps just a few centuries before these people were driven back to the arctic coast where they established what we recognize archaeologically as the Dorset Culture. The warring intruders who replaced them became known as the Taltheilei Shale Tradition. While the Taltheilei Shale Tradition grew, the Microblade Culture gradually died out. Yet there are traces to indicate that Taltheilei Shale may have grown out of the Microblade Culture — specifically, a portion of it located in the southwest corner of the Mackenzie District of the Northwest Territories. Thus the implication is that the Athapaskans prehistorically sprang from the Taltheilei Shale Tradition which in turn had its roots hypothetically in the Microblade Culture.

At least certain Athapaskan tribes must have possessed an inner desire for a warmer climate and an easier way of life. Several groups did migrate as far as the Southwest United States to become the ancestors of the Apache and Navaho. Even today there is little difference in the language of these two widely separated groups: a fact that suggests a relatively recent split. Another Athapaskan tribe, the Sarci, took up buffalo hunting as a means of existence on the Great Plains, and joined in an alliance with the Blackfeet. There are also pockets of Athapaskan-speaking peoples along the coasts of Oregon and Washington. That fewer migrations were made by Athapaskans in a southeasterly direction is undoubtedly explained by the perennial hostilities of the Algonquin (the Cree in particular), against these tribes.

Among Athapaskans, the family was the functional providing unit, and there was little tribal cohesion. Living in small independent family groups, their life centered around the routine of hunting and fishing. Several of these family units would constitute a band who would exploit a given, well-defined territory, each family having its own section of the band's territory. Only on special occasions would the family groups come together to arrange marriages and to visit. They might also come together to coordinate their efforts on a heavy run of fish or when a large caribou herd entered the territory. Even on these occasions there was no special chief or head. Rather, the most experienced and knowledgeable hunter would take charge of the hunting; the best fisherman would oversee the fishing operations, and so on. Group ostracism was the primary means of coercion, and in the North Country this can indeed be a powerful motivating factor.

The Athapaskans practiced no horticulture, but their land lended itself splendidly to gathering during the summer months. Eggs were eagerly gathered on egg islands from the nests of ducks, geese, shorebirds, gulls and terns that came to the tundra each season. Blueberries, low and high-bush cranberries, saskatoon or service berries and currants were picked during the brief summer.

Shelters were for the most part tipi-shaped pole frames covered with caribou skins and bark. Brush covered lean-tos were also used. Subterranean dwellings, undoubtedly Eskimo influenced, were present in western regions. Most implements were of bone, wood, or musk ox horn. Storage containers were fashioned from birch bark.

Stone blades were typically made of quartz but were not used to a great extent. The area around the Coppermine River produced copper nuggets which were hammered into spear and arrow points. Both the finished points and the raw copper were valuable trade commodities among all groups of Indians. Willow bast, sinew, and thin strips of caribou hide called babiche were made into cordage. Used for a multitude of purposes, including bags, nets, and webbing for snowshoes, babiche was a major feature of Athapaskan technology. Nets made of babiche did become slippery when wet and stretched: faults not shared with nets made of cordage from willow inner bark.

Watercraft were essentially birchbark canoes sewn with spruce root and sealed with pine pitch. The frames were of spruce. The Slave Indians along the southern shore of Great Slave Lake used spruce or cottonwood bark instead of birch. Moosehide craft have been noted, and, where Eskimo influence was strong, other types of skin-covered canoes may also have been used. Snowshoes comprised the primary means of winter travel except among the Carriers who had none. Dog sleds were not used in the pre-contact era except among those tribes considerably influenced by the neighboring Eskimos. Even then it was not characteristically a dog team as such, replete with a lead dog and harnesses, but rather a dog or two leashed to a load on skids or toboggan-like vehicle.

Clothing reflected the regional environment, but basically garments were made from caribou skins. There was some decoration utilizing bird and porcupine quills and moosehair embroidery. Long fringe borders typified some central Athapaskan garments. Perhaps this was a Western Plains influence. The Hares, true to their tribal name, used a lot of rabbit skins for clothing. These pelts were cut into thin strips, tied end to end, and then woven into garments.

Child-rearing among Athapaskans was done with an eye toward training future providers. Corporal punishment was unheard of, and children's play became their work. A boy at an early age was presented with a tiny bow and set of arrows. It was not a toy, but a real functioning bow on a miniature scale. He would then be sent to search a ridge just in back of the camp with all of the graveness and earnestness that his father would receive when embarking on a hunt. When he returned to camp with a small bird or ground squirrel, he was met by the whole band who was anxious to hear of his adventures, and who lavished great praise and adulation on the lad for accomplishing this feat. Should he return empty-handed, the same scoffing and ridicule earned by an unsuccessful adult hunter was bestowed upon the boy. Cooking, tending the fire, working with hides and other traditional female tasks were incorporated into the females' play at a very young age as well.

For the Athapaskans, the arduous task of surviving forbade the luxury of extensive artistic endeavors. Few works of art such as carvings were created for the sake of art itself. It was utilitarian items that were occasionally decorated with quillwork, or as in the case of birchbark containers, had their surfaces etched. Perhaps the Indians' greatest artistic expression was through their stories and songs. This was an art-form that lent itself well to long, cold nights in a dark shelter, and one that did not have to be abandoned on the family's hunting forays.

A land that could display such cruelty with its cold winters, long periods of darkness, extreme loneliness and almost perpetual hardships led to strong supernatural beliefs among the Athapaskans and Algonquins. It was not an organized religion but rather the belief in a series of mischievous demons and spirits that dwelt in certain lakes, lurked in rapids, woods or hills and rode on some winds. Each of these spirits had its attendant taboos and was treated with respect and caution. Most subarctic dwellers were a somewhat timorous people and were constantly haunted and held in sway by such mysteries. Among the most feared of ghosts was the legendary Algonquin *windigos* or human beings who had eaten human flesh and been transformed into horrible man-eating giants with lipless mouths, eyes floating in blood and whose footprints in the snow were soaked in blood. Some religious figures, or Shamans, were thought to have limited powers in dealing with certain of these spirits.

Caribou Hunting

The existence of man in the subarctic depended on several animal species — but none was more important than the caribou. Known at least to the Chipewyan as *ethen*, the caribou in their uncountable numbers were a virtual river of life to the inhabitants of this land. Like the buffalo of the Plains Indians and the salmon of the northwest coast dwellers, the caribou was critical to subarctic survival in most areas. Its seasonal appearance at predicted locations during migration meant life for the people. Non-appearance due to the occasional shifts in migration patterns or, in historical times, because of depleted numbers, meant likely starvation during the long, hard winter.

Ethen, as the Indians called the caribou, seemed to be perpetually moving back and forth across the great expanse of tundra. Pulled first north and then south by the change of seasons, they trotted with their heads tossed back in a strange, stiff-legged gait exclusive to this species. They pranced over the vast tundra plains and across the rolling hills, filed through mountain passes and swam across rivers and lakes in their path. In the spring migration they sought their ancestral calving grounds to the north, the gestating females preceding the bulls by several days. In the fall they migrated to the taiga country in the south to winter amidst the relative protection of those stunted forests. When the welcome cry of *"ethen!"* was heard, the camp immediately became a scene of great excitement: men scurrying for their weapons, women shouting the direction of the game and children running to higher ridges to watch the herds. To see this migratory river of tens of thousands of caribou is to witness life at an elemental level. Theirs is an irresistible urge, as ancient as the species itself, to make biannual forays across the great Barrens to assure the existence of their progeny. It is this twice yearly migration, that assures the Indians' existence.

Caribou are grazers and it is the propensity of such a large herd to overgraze an area that necessitates their nomadic existence. The margin of survival is thin in the subarctic and overgrazing cannot be tolerated. Even young caribou seem to be born with an insatiable wanderlust; and from the time they are only a few hours old caribou calves are capable of maintaining a steady, purposeful gait for long distances behind their mothers.

The most crucial caribou hunt was during the fall migration. Various methods and devices were used depending on features of the terrain and cultural tradition. The Kutchin, Han, and several others employed a circular impoundment with converging wings leading into it just as did many of the Plains tribes for buffalo. Samuel Hearne, an explorer for the Hudson Bay Company, on his overland trek in 1771 to explore the Coppermine River, noted that one of these pounds was a full mile (1.6 kilometer) in circumference. The vertical posts of the pound were permanent structures, and the brush barrier woven between the posts was repaired each summer in preparation for the fall hunt. The converging wings that funneled the caribou into the pound were stone cairns, spaced increasingly close together near the mouth of the enclosure. Sometimes their effectiveness was enhanced by poles with bird wings tied to them which waved in the breeze. Snares might be set inside the pound or at openings left in the wall of the pound. As animals were removed from these and the snares reset, it would be just a short while until another animal from the milling herd within was caught.

Caribou drift fences were extremely effective. A long fence made of spruce poles and interwoven brush would be built across the tundra. Growing trees were utilized where possible. At intervals, an opening, just large enough for a single caribou to pass through, was left. A cross bar would be placed over the top of the opening, and from this a hide noose dangled down in which the caribou was caught.

Solitary snares were also set at likely crossings, but toss poles were used rather than the more familiar spring pole. The latter could be prematurely sprung by the fierce arctic winds. The poles would lose their spring due to the cold. Toss poles needed to be set where some timber was present. These traps were commonly used in Alaska and combined the principles of a deadfall and a noose. The noose was draped over the limb of a tree and left dangling in the path of the caribou. The main noose line passed through a hole in the upper end of a log propped diagonally against a tree and then tied to the tree itself. The force of the caribou hitting the noose tripped the log. The fall of the log tightened the noose about the caribou. The chance of an animal coming into the vicinity of the snare was increased by using a piece of frozen urine from either a man or a dog. Craving the salt, caribou would abandon all caution to get to this morsel. Wolves have been seen using this ploy by urinating near a snow hummock and then lying concealed nearby waiting for caribou to be lured in.

The techniques described so far all required logs or standing trees for their construction. Throughout much of the Barrens, pockets of trees were plentiful enough to suffice for these purposes. However, in truly treeless portions, other methods had to be used. Hunters on

A bull caribou has become entangled in a babiche snare left in an opening in a drift fence.

snowshoes could outrun animals in deep snow. This, too, was largely a method of forested areas as there was seldom enough deep snow on the open tundra to slow the caribou's speed. Ambush tactics were usually successful, especially if the hunters camouflaged themselves under caribou hides and wore antlers. Over the hundreds of miles of caribou migration, the older and weaker animals would gradually slip toward the back of the herd. These animals, un-suspectingly covering ground already traversed by the rest of the herd, were the ones that ambush tactics worked best on.

Primitive game calls, as well, were successfully used on caribou. Naturalists have dissected caribou legs over the years to·determine what it is about the bone structure of their ankles that makes the characteristic clicking noise when they walk. A herd of caribou passing sounds like an orchestra of castanets. A set of antler tips attached to thongs would make a clicking sound when jiggled and often was effective in luring a herd of caribou to within a hunter's range. Bows and arrows and bone or stone-tipped spears thrown from an atlatl were the Indians' weapons. The bows were made from wood or fashioned from sections of musk ox horn or caribou antler ingeniously spliced together and perhaps backed with sinew.

Migrating caribou had favorite river and lake crossings they used year after year. The people of *ethen* were intimately familiar with these, and after the migration was underway, would lie in wait in their canoes around a point of land so as to be out of sight. Sometimes a few appropriately placed stone cairns might prompt the herd into crossing at a more advantageous spot for the hunters where the animals' swim was longer or the water deeper. The swimming caribou were greatly disadvantaged and could be easily overcome and slaughtered with bows, clubs or lances. The Indians also used poles with a hide noose on the end to entangle the caribou's antlers, forcing their head

Athapaskans were presented with a prime opportunity to make a major caribou harvest when the animals were forced to make a lake or river crossing on their migration route.

A Naskapi hunter has had a successful caribou hunt.

underwater and drowning the animal. To keep the dispatched caribou from sinking, the hunters would cunningly hook a foreleg behind the antlers (caribou are the only members of the deer family whose females also regularly sport antlers, small though they may be) in such a way that the neck was cocked back and the mouth and nostrils would float above the water surface. The few caribou that might gain the shore were usually mortally wounded and too weak to flee. After the slaughter was finished, the men would tow the floating bodies to the shore. Women and children would come down and the butchering would begin. The meat was cut into long thin strips and dried to make jerky.

If the caribou should inexplicably change their migration route and not show up at the expected crossings, the band would have to hurriedly pack the tanned hides that covered their shelters, their few belongings, and set off in hopes of intercepting the herd. Home was wherever *ethen* provided sustenance.

The hunt for caribou during their fall migration may have been the most important for survival purposes; but certainly the spring migration must have been the most anticipated after having endured a long winter. The thud of thousands of hooves crossing the ice of the frozen river and then clacking against the rocks scattered along the shoreline, the low coughing grunts of the cows: these sounds fracturing the blackness of the subarctic night, told the hunters in the shelters of their winter camp along the river that spring was near. *Ethen* had returned to the land.

The Cree did not have access to the migrating barrenground caribou. Their land was too far south. They depended on the more solitary woodland caribou with its smaller herds. The great migrations did not occur among these caribou, and they were more permanent residents of Algonquin land. Snares and ambush methods were the favored techniques. During the summer months, the cows would calve on islands in the lakes, presumably to escape wolf predation. At this time, cows would frequently be seen swimming from one island to another with their calf right behind. The hollow hairs of the caribou made them extremely buoyant, and in addition each hair was club-shaped, thicker at the tip than at the base, which trapped even more air next to the hide. These island-hopping caribou offered the Cree an easy kill at a time when the animals were quite scattered.

Hunting
other Large Game

Moose, being browsing animals, would feed mostly on the shoots and leaves of willow, birch and aspen. They were quite common in most boreal forest areas, as well as those sections of tundra with rivers therefore offering this type of forage. All the subarctic tribes had moose in their land and most were expert at hunting them. They knew where every likely habitat was to be found: long willow stands in the bend of a river, in grassy meadows or around small shallow lakes where the animals graze on sedges, horsetail and pond weeds. Canadian Indians used birch bark calls and dried scapulas to attract moose during the rut.

Both the Athapaskans and the Algonquins were adept at tracking moose and stalking to within bow and arrow range. As they traveled along rivers, they watched the muddy and sandy banks for tracks. These hunters were masterly at determining the age of a track and the sex, size, and condition of the animal that made it. If a track was sharp in outline and remained as moist as the surrounding earth, it was probably fresh. Older tracks dried out around

A Cree uses his birch bark call for moose.

their edges. Of course such observations had to be estimated taking into account warmth and sunniness of the day. Tracks higher up on a river bank or lake shore might gradually fill with ground water seeping in from below. Such tracks were probably old. Conversely, tracks closer to the water's edge might immediately fill with water. Here, if the water filling the spoor was murky, it had probably just been made. Clear water in the track would indicate an elapse of sufficient time for the muddiness to subside.

Tracking in snow presented a different set of problems. Again, the subarctic hunter was not interested in tracks that were over two days old, but especially wanted to find tracks made the previous night. Newly-made tracks were as fresh as the surrounding snow. In only a matter of hours a track in snow started to develop a crust, first around the top and later near the bottom. This hardness was usually tested by stepping in a few tracks to see how much pressure was needed to break the crust.

Excrement left by the moose was also an excellent indicator of time elapsed since the animal passed through. Fresh moose droppings were soft and dark brown in color. As they froze, the color changed to a lighter brown. The rapidity of these changes depended on the air temperature.

The job of tracking was facilitated by having a fair idea of where the moose was heading, based on the hunter's knowledge of the local topography. The dank, musky odor of a moose, particularly during the rut, was prevalent and frequently forewarned the hunter of a moose's proximity.

Moose were clever at guarding their tracks. They usually doubled back downwind from their own trail before bedding down. The scent of any animal following them would then drift down to where they were lying and alert them. Immediately upon hearing any sound in their vicinity or on their back trail, a moose would circle to get downwind so they could identify the intruder by scent. The wise Indian hunter therefore frequently searched downwind for a moose that he had frightened. Better yet, if two hunters were stalking a moose, one might be left on the back trail while the other continued his pursuit. The stationary hunter frequently was presented the best shot as the moose circled to get downwind. Another predictable moose reaction was for a cow and calf to return to the area in which they were last together before being frightened away. A hunter who waited at this location was frequently successful.

Deep snow, particularly if it was covered with a crust, was a serious adversory to all the large ungulates. Their sharp hooves, driven by the weight of huge bodies, broke through the thin surface crust and left the animals floundering up to their bellies in snow. The crust, however, may easily support a pack of wolves who could quickly close in on the mired animal. Indians of the Western Plains noted this phenomenon with the buffalo, as did the Indians of the Eastern forests and subarctic areas with moose. Each of these groups of hunters adapted this behavioral interaction to their own form of human predation. The Athapaskans and Algonquins used their dogs to chase moose in deep snow while they followed on snowshoes with their bows and spears.

National Museum of Canada, Ottawa

A latter day Carrier Indian scrapes a small summer moose hide.

In wintertime communal moose drives were frequently undertaken. The scrub willow-covered islands in rivers were particularly good locations for these. Moose frequently wintered on such islands and tracks on, or leading to, the island indicated whether or not it was occupied. If the island was closer to one shore of the river, it was certain that this would be the favored direction for the moose to flush and escape the drivers. Hunters would station themselves along this side of the island where their view was optimal, and they could get the closest shot.

Snaring was perhaps accountable for even more moose than the traditional tracking, stalking, driving and calling methods. The essential consideration was to locate the babiche snare in a narrow opening in the brush where the moose was forced to walk into the trap rather than around it.

Musk oxen were occasionally hunted in the far north for hides, horns and meat. Their habitat was almost beyond the home territory of most tribes, and these animals were usually hunted on special trips, the hunters lingering no longer than necessary in that harsh, windswept environment. With the exception of man, wolves were about the only predators with which musk ox needed to concern themselves. They displayed a unique form of protection when attacked. Not unlike wagon trains in western movies forming a circle for protection against attacking Indians, musk oxen would back their rumps up to each other and present their fierce horns and front hooves to the marauding wolf pack. Such a standoff afforded a better defense than trying to run away with the much quicker wolves snapping at their hamstrings. Indian hunters were able to turn this defense posture to their advantage by using dogs to get the musk ox to bunch and make a stand. Then it was not difficult to get within bow range and make a kill.

Both black and grizzly bears inhabit Canada's interior.

It is likely that the actual contribution of these species to the Athapaskan and Algonquin economies was not as great as the role they played in the minds of the people.

The grizzly in particular was an awesome opponent to encounter with primitive weapons. These animals were more or less free roamers of the far north tundra country, and den in large jumbles of glacier-deposited rocks called pingos. In Canada, unlike further south in the eastern hardwood forests, the black bear was a true hibernator. The grizzly, on the other hand, seemed to take hibernation much less seriously. They would not plug the entrance to their dens as black bears did, leaving it open so they might come out and wander around in mid-winter. The lightness of their stupor while in the den was proven by the savage growl that usually emanated when a human approached too closely. The black bear, on the other hand, spent the winter in an almost anesthetized state.

The best time to kill either black or grizzly bears was while they were in their dens. Hunters often stumbled onto bear dens by accident when they were traveling at any time of year. They knew, depending on the weather, that black bears would start preparing and frequenting their dens by late September. Grizzlies prepared much later, usually November or December. About this time each year, a hunter would start checking the dens he knew about to see if they were occupied. Bears might remain active in the near vicinity of their dens before actually entering them, digging up moss and dirt in search of roots. This was usually a sure indication that a den nearby would soon be occupied. These signs and the dens themselves were much harder to find once snow has fallen.

Black bears, being deeper hibernators, took considerable pains in preparing their den. They would line the interior of their lair with grass and moss from the surrounding area. Once inside, this same material would be used to plug the entrance. Only a small breathing vent would be left, and after snow has fallen this would be ringed with rime, the frozen condensation from the bears breath. White hoarfrost would form on some of the vegetation for a few feet around the breathing hole and such a sign, visible for a short distance, might alert a hunter to the presence of a den after other signs had been obliterated by snow.

Once a den was located, the next task was to determine if it was occupied and in which direction the cavity ran. Rime around a breathing hole clearly indicated habitation. If this was lacking, the Indian hunter might have to probe the recesses of the lair with a pole to feel for the bear and to assess the depth and direction of the den. This sounding might provoke the bear into moving, which would be readily felt with the pole. If not, he might have to push the probe firmly against what he thought was the body of the bear and feel for its chest cavity to move in slow, rythmic respiration. Sometimes this breathing could be heard if the hunter placed his ear close to the opening.

After the bear's position in the den was determined, there were two ways to kill it. One was to keep agitating the animal with the probe until it stuporously blundered forth and could be shot or speared. The other alternative was to plug the entrance with poles or logs, perhaps even tying them in place, so the bear could not escape. The Indian would then dig down through the roof of the den onto the bear and shoot or spear it there. If the interior of the den was quite dark, a scattering of snow on the animal might reflect enough light to identify a lethal place to shoot an arrow or thrust a spear. The hole was then enlarged further and the slain bear dragged out.

Tender grasses along lakes and rivers were some of the first green vegetation to appear in the spring. Black bears, particularly hungry when they emerged from their dens, came down to the water's edge to eat this tender new growth. This was an ideal time to hunt from a boat. In primitive times, these animals were rather oblivious to danger approaching from the water and a very close approach could be made.

Black bears would tree when chased by a pack of dogs but woe to the dog pack that tried this with a grizzly. In certain instances, a call could be effectively used. If fresh bear signs were present, but the exact location of the bear not known, the hunter could conceal himself and imitate the call of a raven. The call told the bear the ravens had located carrion and the animal was certain to check it out.

Pitfalls and deadfalls were used for black bears, but these devices could not be constructed to contain a grizzly. Snares, however, were used for both species of bears. Fall was the best time for using snares because not only were bears fat at this time, but they also tended to wander along rather well-defined trails. The snares were made from braided strands of babiche and were amazingly strong. The idea was to place them on a bear trail where the path narrowed because of the underbrush and the set could not be side-stepped. A truly ideal location was where a log had fallen across the trail and the bear was forced to pass underneath. In such a situation the snare was tethered to the log itself and the loop could be made to fill the whole passage.

Hunting Small Game

The Cree around James Bay used clever funnel traps for beaver. The traps were made of slender spruce staves lashed to hoops. The larger end easily permitted the passage of the beaver, but the smaller end was large enough for only the beaver's head. Furthermore, the springy tips of the staves extending beyond the last hoop on this small end would catch the beaver at the base of the skull and prevent it from withdrawing its head. A break was

Two Cree hunters take a drowned beaver from a funnel trap that had been placed in a break made in their dam.

made in a beaver dam and the funnel trap placed in the water pouring through this gap. The smaller end pointed downstream. The beaver, coming to investigate the break in the dam, would swim into the funnel, be unable to pull its head back out and would drown. A unique type of deadfall trap was used by the Algonquins and some Athapaskans for beaver. Relying on a triggering device, such as the classic "figure 4", to be activated, the trap consisted not of just a dead weight to pin the animal, but employed a weighted spear that fell vertically to impale the beaver. Such a deadfall could be used over burrows going up under the bank. The Algonquins also used various other methods of hunting and trapping beaver practiced by Eastern Woodland tribes.

One of the first rites of spring was the muskrat hunt. They were either caught in snares set in runways or shot with bows and arrows. The pelts were fashioned into a number of garments and the carcasses were either stone-boiled in birch bark containers or roasted on a stick over an open fire. Even today, tribes living in the Mackenzie River Valley participate in an annual spring muskrat hunt.

Pitfalls were the type of trap most successful with wolves, and the Cree devised a particularly ingenious variation capable of capturing several in a single night. The top of the trap was covered by a revolving trap door. Each side of the door had a piece of raw meat tied to it. When a wolf approached the bait, the animal's weight revolved the pivoting door and dumped the wolf inside. Whichever side of the door turned up would still have bait in place, ready for the next wolf. After the first two wolves were caught in this manner, their vicious fighting and snapping would attract more wolves until the pit was full. Further north, perma-frost hindered the digging of pitfalls, so tower traps were constructed to operate on the same principle. In essence a negative pitfall, these were cylindrical towers built of stones with a ramp leading to an unobtainable bait at the top. Foxes were particularly susceptible to tower traps. These devices were used primarily by the Ingalik and Koyukon, who borrowed heavily from the Eskimo culture.

Many arctic animals underwent great natural variations in their population. The smaller mammals particularly, such as snowshoe hares, foxes, and lemmings, appeared to vacillate between incredible abundance and near extinction. It seemed at times to be almost by divine providence in favour of the subarctic hunters that these cycles did not ebb for all species the same year. If moose were scarce, perhaps there would be a good fishing season. If the caribou migration was not as predicted, there might have been an up-cycle of snowshoe hares that enabled the Indians to continue to provide. Undoubtedly in primitive times there were lean winters when Indian families survived only because there were snowshoe hares to snare. In the cold of the subarctic, sometimes even the rabbits were not enough. Such a cold climate demanded ample body fat stores to provide calories for warmth and necessary activities. This human body fat reserve, or the absence of it, became crucial to survival under conditions of near starvation. Rabbit meat, as well as some other types, was extremely lean. It was of low nutritional density. Regardless of the number of rabbits one might eat, if other fatty meat was not available, sufficient calories might not be consumed to prevent starvation. People of the North still speak of "rabbit starvation" in reference to this condition. Prehistoric peoples probably also recognized this situation and strived to supplement their winter diets with fat-rich meats such as caribou, moose, bear, trout or salmon.

Snares were set in rabbit trails. These were discovered by noting where grass was parted and ground litter or snow was well matted down. Such trails were used by hares all year long and were worn down enough to be clearly defined. The nooses were made of braided sinew, and usually rubbed with jack pine to kill human scent. Both spring poles and toss-pole styles of snares were utilized. The spring pole had the advantage of immediately choking the animal to death so it could not chew through the sinew, and it also lifted the animal off the ground away from scavengers. Ravens were a particular nuisance and could pick a rabbit bare to the bones in a few hours. Furthermore, these intelligent birds would soon learn the entire line of snares and regularly visit each of the sets. Spring-pole snares were a little bit more difficult to set however, and they could not be used in very cold weather because the frozen wood lacked sufficient spring.

Snowshoe hares were seldom shot in winter because they were so well camouflaged in the snow. One successful method however, was to cut a number of birch or willow branches and pile them in a row or stack. Hares were attracted to the fresh feed, particularly if the grass was covered and yet the snow was not deep enough for the animals to reach the tender lowest branches of trees and bushes. The hunter would go to that place in the evening with his bow and stunning arrows and wait for them to appear.

Late in the winter hares must have anticipated spring almost as much as the Indians did because they came out of their concealing hollows to soak up the low rays of the sun. They were particularly common on clear days this time of year along lake or river banks that had the most exposure to the sun. Even women and children joined men on the hunt now, and their quest was made easier by the fact the hares were starting to turn brown again making them more visible. They basked so contentedly that they were easily approached to within bow and arrow range. Even if a rabbit did start to hop off into the brush, a series of soft short whistles would entice it to pause and stand up on its hind feet, offering an excellent shot. Netted babiche hunting bags were carried over the shoulder to carry the game in.

Communal rabbit drives were carried out in the winter. Isolated willow stands, such as on islands, were ideal locations for these. A series of snares or perhaps a long sinew net would be set at the end of the drive. Each driver would zigzag across the area, covering all the ground between himself and the hunter next to him. Any rabbit that escaped the snares and nets was shot by a line of hunters in a clearing at the end of the drive.

In prosperous times, hares were a flavorful supplement; in hard times they were sometimes crucial for survival. The soft fur was used as insoles for moccasins and as a liner for mittens.

Porcupines were frequently encountered and easily killed. They were prepared by throwing the entire carcass into a fire, and burning all the quills off. The few quills that remained were scraped off with a stick. The animal was then boiled, charred skin and all. These fat animals, flavored with the burnt skin, were considered a delicacy.

Gopher snares were made from strips of eagle feather rib. These were made with a running-slip knot and bound to a small twig along the standing portion. The twig acted as a toggle and also served as a tie for a length of babiche. These were set at the entrances to gopher burrows with a bent willow stick serving as the spring.

Waterfowl Hunting

Waterfowl were stalked and shot from blinds with blunt-tipped stunning arrows. Most resident-nesting waterfowl underwent a molt about mid-summer. During this time, all wing flight feathers were shed and while in this "eclipse" plumage the birds were rendered temporarily incapable of flight and easily caught by hunters using willow fiber, sinew or babiche nets. The birds could even be run down on land and caught by hand. Ptarmigan were caught in snares set in openings left in brush fences.

Canada geese, as well as snow geese, were captured by the Cree around Hudson Bay with a trench trap. It consisted of a simple trench approximately 15 feet (4.5 meters) long, 25 inches (64 centimeters) deep and 16 inches (41 centimeters) wide with the floor at both ends sloping up to the ground level. The trench was baited with wild rice. Geese would fly in and begin eating the grain around the ends of the trap and then on into the trench. Indian hunters, who had been hiding in wait nearby, would dash from their cover to seize the birds and to wring their necks. The geese could not immediately fly away because they did not have enough room in the narrow trench to open their wings. All of the Algonquin tribes were masters at calling geese and further enhanced their efforts with crude but effective land decoys made of mud, a pile of rocks or a hummock of moss. A roughly carved pine stick with a knot made an admirable head and neck and some additional touches of realism, consisting of feathers stuck in the sides to look like wings, were sometimes used. Of course, the most realistic decoys of all were previously slaughtered geese, their heads propped up by a forked stick.

Whitefronted geese follow a grain trail into the confines of a trench trap. Here, unable to open their wings, they will be easy prey for the concealed hunters.

A Naskapi hunter uses a blunt-tipped stunning arrow on waterfowl.

An Ingalik man tends his trap for dog salmon near Anvik, Alaska on the Yukon River. He is scaring fish to the back of the trap before lifting it.

Fishing

Certain western Athapaskan tribes such as the Koyukon and Carrier had access to salmon streams, and the dependable abundance of fish negated the need for the nomadic existence of other Athapaskans. The methods used to harvest salmon were learned from Northwest Coast neighbors, with few alterations. Over the remainder of the culture area, summer camps were made on islands in the larger lakes that had traditionally offered good fishing. Hopefully, these island locations also offered some degree of reprieve from the multitude of black flies and mosquitoes that infested the area at this time of year.

In the early summer, willow fiber nets were strung across small feeder streams for the sucker run. Later, larger versions of these nets, used in gill-net fashion, were set off points and across bays for lake trout. In the fall, whitefish spawned on the lake shoals and in tributary streams. Basket traps made of spruce staves lashed to hoops with spruce roots were formed in a conical shape and fitted one inside the other. These two-piece traps were used in conjunction with weirs for whitefish when concentrated during spawning. Fish not prepared fresh were smoked or dried and cached for winter use.

Considerable fishing was done through the winter ice before it became too thick. Fish decoys were carved out of ivory or bone and jigged enticingly through a hole in the ice. In this manner pike and trout were lured within spearing range. Lures of bone and ivory, with barbs attached, were also jigged and when a fish was excitedly swimming about nosing the lure, a sudden jerk hooked them in the belly or under the jaw. Spruce trees, with boughs intact, were shoved vertically through holes cut in river ice to herd white fish over a net with a wooden frame on the bottom. A fisherman, head covered with a piece of caribou hide so he could see into the murky depths, would quickly raise the framed net when a school of whitefish passed over it. Any solitary whitefish could easily swim through the spruce tree barrier but, perceiving safety in numbers, they remained intact as a school and swam in group fashion through the opening left for them with the net underneath. In the lakes, gill nets stretched over pole-frames were lowered vertically through slots cut in the ice, and were effective in catching lake trout.

Smithsonian Institution — Photo by Rev. John Wight Chapman, Anvik, Alaska 1898

An Ingalik man removes fish from a basket trap that is used through the ice.

National Museum of Canada, Ottawa

**Bark house for smoking fish
in British Columbia.
Possibly Sekani.**

Smithsonian Institution — Photo by Rev. John Wight Chapman 1903

**Dog salmon dry on a rack in an Ingalik camp near Anvik, Alaska. The
dog salmon-run in this region starts about the middle of June and
lasts a month.**

157

Not unlike many areas of North America, the catalyst bringing Caucasian and Indian together in the subarctic was the quest for furs. The Hudson Bay Company was established on the western shore of Hudson Bay in 1670. Trader-explorers like Alexander Mackenzie, Samuel Hearne, David Thompson, Simon Fraser, and Peter Pond opened the interior of Canada to the fur trade. The Russian fur trade in Alaska was largely limited to the coasts and few significant inland excursions were made. The tribes of the Alaskan interior were the last to be visited and influenced by the whites. The Canadian traders were not desirous of changing the natives or taking their land. They wanted only furs because the European demand was insatiable. At first, the Indians seemed to fit nicely into the plan; given steel traps they could secure the furs and in turn they wanted the knives, rifles, pots, staples and other trade items offered. But the process of destruction was inevitable. First there were the invisible invaders: smallpox, alcoholism, and other scourges of the white man; but the true culprit was the change in lifestyle that followed. No longer were caribou hunted as a primary means of existence. Rather, a seemingly easier lifestyle was adopted of trapping beaver, fox, and other furbearers, and then trading for necessities. Diets changed as flour, tea, and sugar supplemented meat, fish and berries. At first, annual cycles of hunting and fishing activities were adjusted to accommodate long trips to trading posts to obtain goods they now considered indispensable. Later, old ways and productive hunting areas were totally abandoned for areas closer to trading routes and posts. The Indians became enslaved to the white fur trade.

Wanton waste of caribou increased dramatically. Caribou which had once fed humans were slaughtered to feed sled dogs now necessary to transport bales of furs. Some unscrupulous traders encouraged the wholesale slaughter of caribou by trading a box of ammunition for a certain number of caribou tongues. Accounting was certainly not an asset of the subarctic Indians, and the white man exploited this weakness to accumulate an indebtedness to the trader and a means of selling ammunition. Meanwhile, thousands of caribou carcasses, so easily killed with the newly acquired rifles, rotted on the tundra.

The vagaries of the fur trade were far more fickle than the natural fluctuations of the moose population, the runs of fish or the migrations of the caribou in earlier times. The fox population was cyclical, tied to that of rodents. Beaver were over-trapped and disappeared from many areas. Fur market prices became capricious. Traders in the interior who had fostered an addiction for trade goods among their Indian clients pulled out during lean times. Notations from the journal of Richard King at Fort Resolution in the 1800's vividly describe the cruel starvation that came to one Chipewyan band:

"The feeble gait of the torpid and downcast father — the piercing and sepulchral cry of the mother — the infant clinging by a parched mouth to a withered breast, faintly moaning through its nostrils — the passive child, calmly awaiting its doom — the faithful dog, destroyed and consumed — the caribou robe dwindling almost to nothing — can give but a very inadequate idea of their suffering."

The people of *ethen* became people of the steel trap, and this led to their demise as the freely wandering hunters of the north country.

Grizzly bear Browarny Photographics Ltd.

Hunters
of the Buffalo

The American Indian: he chases buffalo on horseback, wears feathered war bonnets and beaded moccasins, lives in a tipi, and smokes a peace pipe. This cursory and inadequate description represents the stereotypic view of the Indians held by most Europeans and Americans. Even among the Plains Culture which gave rise to this archetypal Indian of movies, comics and novels, there is no typical Indian. The dour, stoic warrior with his aquiline nose and a language consisting mostly of dull-witted "hows," "ughs" and words ending in the suffix "um" is the feeble product of dramatists and romanticists. Many of the Indians' material belongings such as horses, guns and glass beads that helped to make the Western Plains Indian the so-called epitome of all that is "Indian" were actually acquired from the white man.

The Western Plains extend from the Mississippi to the base of the Rockies and from the southwest cactus country north to the conifer forests of Canada. Contained within this sizable area are several sub-ecosystems blending indistinguishably one into another. The eastern portion, with its greater rainfall, is the long-grass prairie. This blends into the short-grass prairie to the west and southwest.

The buffalo — the life-blood of the Plains Indian

This was the land of the buffalo: a huge, black inland sea of living beasts. The staggeringly huge biomass of the herds taxed the descriptive powers of early explorers. "In numbers numberless" and "like fishes in the sea" were the trite images recorded in their journals. Their individual size was awesome, their numbers vast, and their distribution wide. A mature bull might stand seven feet (2 meters) at the shoulder and weigh as much as 2,000 pounds (907 kilograms). Buffalo were gregarious animals amassing in herds of both sexes and all ages for protection. While predatory wolf packs were constantly skirting the edge of the herd to prey on young and weak animals, no enemy — except man — could challenge this herd as a whole.

The long-horned bison (*Bison antiquus*) was the first buffalo to be hunted by the Paleo hunters on the plains. Larger even than the modern American Bison (*Bison bison*), this species became extinct about 25,000 years ago for reasons that are still uncertain. The vacuum the extinction of these large ungulates produced on the Plains was filled by a gradual northward migration of the smaller American Bison from Mexico.

Buffalo were indispensable to the Plains Indians, particularly following the advent of horses, providing all necessary materials for clothing and shelter, food and a wide array of luxury items of considerable aesthetic value.

The meat of the buffalo had a beef-like quality. When prepared fresh, it was roasted, stewed, broiled, or eaten raw. Uncooked organs were particularly relished, and the task of butchering was made more enjoyable by snacking on the still-warm liver, kidneys, eyes and testicles. The chewy gristle-like hooves of unborn calves were especially savory morsels. The Blackfeet held the taste of raw liver in high esteem and felt that its palatability was further enhanced by a thin spreading of bile from the gallbladder. Though eating raw entrails was disdained by a few tribes such as the Kutenai, most Plains Indians eagerly feasted on

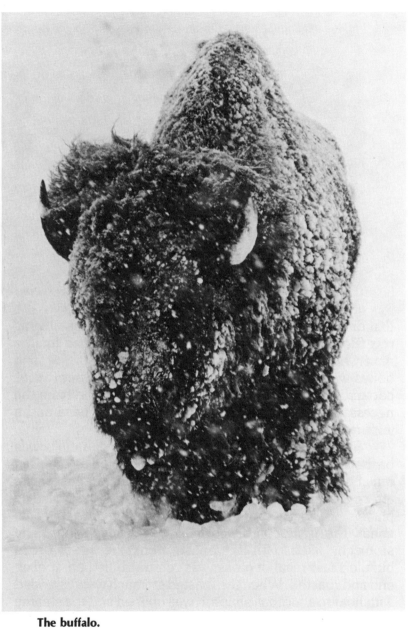

The buffalo.

The buffalo shared the plains and foothills with many other species of big game including elk.

the organs. The tongue was perhaps the most highly regarded piece of meat and was usually reserved for the man who had slain the animal. The marrow of the long bones was extracted and eaten with fervor, either raw or cooked. The Indians also drank the warm blood from the freshly killed animals and the clotted blood became an important ingredient in soups and puddings.

At the kill site, the frontal bone of the buffalo was bashed in with a stone maul so the brains could be scooped out and mixed with the blood that pooled in the chest cavity after butchering. This concoction was then stone-boiled by placing hot rocks in the cauldron formed by the rib cage. When the mixture congealed it was ready to eat. The stomach, filled with the mash from the herbivorous buffalo's last meal of grass, was removed, tied off at each end and roasted. When the roasted stomach was distended with heat to a football shape, it was opened and the steamy contents devoured. The kill might have taken place a long

distance from a water source, and the parched throats of thirsty hunters were relieved by cutting off the nipples of lactating udders and drinking the tepid milk.

In the spring and summer, bulls were preferred for consumption since the cows were nursing and usually quite emaciated. During the fall and winter, cows carried the choice meat and, along with yearling calves, were considered the most tender.

Although feasting on cooked fresh meat and raw organs after a kill was a satisfying and joyous occasion for the Plains Indian, of more importance to year-round survival was the meat they could preserve and store. Strips of thinly-sliced raw flesh were draped over pole frames serving the dual purpose of keeping the meat away from the hungry dogs and allowing the dry air to desiccate the flesh. The smoke from a smouldering fire under the meat rack added its preserving qualities and the result was jerky. This dehydrated meat was very light, easily transported and remarkably resistant to spoilage.

It was the culinary expertise of the Plains Indians that developed that marvelous wilderness staple, pemmican, which later became so important to white frontiersmen.

Alberta Provincial Government

A Blackfoot woman tends meat smoking on a pole frame.

Pemmican had all the qualities of transportability and preservability of jerky, except to a greater degree, and was of much higher nutritional quality. Pemmican was made from jerky that had been pounded with a stone maul or pemmican pounder. This finely pulverized jerky was placed in a rawhide sack, and marrow fat that had been heated to a liquid consistency was poured over the top. The hot marrow filtered down through the dried chips of meat forming a film around each piece, and acting as a preservative. Sometimes, dried berries and nuts were stirred in to add flavor, but this was thought to interfere with the preservative qualities of the mixture. The sack was then sewn shut and the seams sealed with tallow. Finally, the whole pillow-sized parcel was pounded to an even thickness of about six inches (15 centimeters) for convenient storage and easy portability.

An Asparoke woman scrapes a buffalo hide in front of her tipi.

Next to food, the most important commodity provided by the buffalo was the hide. Two basic tanning processes were utilized. The tough hides of bulls obtained on summer hunts were hard-tanned into what the French called *parfleche*. This stiff material was fashioned into an assortment of rigid vessels, storage containers and war shields. Even when soft-tanned, the summer bull hides were inferior to those taken in the fall and winter and would be utilized for tipi covers, ground covers, implement haftings, saddles and horse trappings, rope, bull boats, snowshoes, dance rattles and other uses where strength and durability were more important than softness and pliancy. Bull hides taken in the fall and winter were soft-tanned with the hair left on for use as blankets and robes. Most inner garments in the wardrobe of Plains Indians such as shirts, leggings, dresses and moccasins were expertly tanned from the skins of cows killed on the late fall and winter hunts. Hides tanned as soft as the finest cloths that Europe could offer were derived from young calves, and these were used for child and infant clothing as well as cradleboard coverings.

The buffalo virtually sustained life for the Plains Indians. Most items they needed were supplied by this one animal. ▶

A Mandan bull boat and paddle. These were typically made from the tough summer hides of bull buffalo.

The remainder of the buffalo carcass was ingeniously employed in the fashioning of an astonishing array of decorative and utilitarian items. Hair was braided into strong rope. The horns were cut and steamed into shape to make ladles and spoons. They also served as cups, heads for ceremonial clubs, tinder boxes and were cut into various types of ornaments. The Crow and Cheyenne possibly made bows from buffalo horns. Hooves and other cartilaginous body parts such as the muzzle, penis and sections of the rib cage were melted down to make glue. Fleshing tools were made from sharpened lower leg bones, and the scapula, when hafted to a handle, made an excellent hoe. Porous bones were used to apply paint to hides. Reinforced rib cages were used as snow sleds, and buffalo teeth were important decorative ornaments. The tendons that attached muscle to bone were dried and made into sinew for thread. Braided strands of sinew were used for bowstrings. Hollow organs such as the stomach, bladder and intestine were fashioned into all sorts of collapsible buckets, saucepans and canteens. A dried scrotum made an admirable water dipper or dance rattle. Hair combs were made from the hard dried skin of a buffalo's tongue. Even dried dung did not escape the practical and innovative eye of the Plains Indian. When burned, these buffalo chips provided a clear, hot flame with little smoke.

Hunting on Foot

Prior to the introduction of horses in the sixteenth century, Plains hunters lived what would be called a semi-nomadic existence. They had a fixed abode for the duration of the winter or longer. These shelters had a wooden frame that was covered with sticks or reeds, and was in turn covered with a layer of sod which afforded excellent year-round insulation. As was the trend among the majority of tribes throughout North America during this period, agriculture played an increasingly important role in the Indians' existence. Methods of raising corn, squash, sunflowers and beans had been learned from other tribes to the southwest who were almost totally dependent upon agriculture.

As soon as the snow melted in the spring, bands of hunters started searching for buffalo on foot. A major slaughter was not carried out, but the hunters hoped a few animals could be killed close to camp as fresh meat was direly needed at this time of year. Before embarking upon the summer hunt, a garden patch was planted. The very young, old, and the sick and infirm were left to tend the crops while the remainder of the camp went out on the hunt that would last for a month or two. In late summer the hunting party returned to their permanent encampment with a few hides and some meat. As soon as the crops were harvested and stored, the long fall hunt began. The buffalo were in their prime at this time of year, and the major kill was made to procure meat and hides for the long winter months ahead. The spoils of the hunt were returned to camp by backpacking and by dog *travois*. This limited both the distance that could be traveled and the amount that could be returned to the permanent camp. Ideally, enough meat could be dried and brought back that, along with the stores of grain, there would be ample supplies for winter. A particularly fortuitous circumstance would be a buffalo herd sharing a valley with the winter encampment. Under such circumstances, an occasional hunting foray might take place. Mostly though, the winter was a time of waiting for the spring thaw. Hopefully, it was not a period of famine.

Impounding was the preferred method of taking buffalo on the Western Plains before the advent of horses. This method was extensively used by the Assiniboine, Blackfeet, Gros Ventre, Crow and Cheyenne. A corral was constructed out of poles and situated in a coulee or clump

Stony Indian Chief from the northern plains. While he is dressed in ceremonial costume, the travois and pack horses played an important role in the band's mobility and ability to follow the moving herds of buffalo.

Dogs were commonly used as beasts of burden before horses were available.

of trees where it was not immediately evident to the shortsighted buffalo. A log ramp covered with sod to resemble the surrounding prairie floor led to the opening of the impoundment. This gradual incline dropped precipitously several feet at the lip of the corral. The drop was enough to prevent the driven beasts from running back out of the trap when they discovered their mistake. The fall was also sufficient to break the legs of the buffalo, and stumps were left standing just inside the corral to increase the

chance of death as the buffalo came pounding in — one on top of another.

Extending out onto the open prairie for a mile (1.6 kilometers) or more were two lines of stations forming a V with the apex at the mouth of the corral. These were constructed of piles of stone or buffalo chips. During an impoundment attempt, these were manned by an Indian with a robe that he might wave to induce the buffalo to stay on their fateful course toward the corral.

The stations were sparsely positioned at the outer limits of the wings: spaced infrequently enough so as not to alert the wary buffalo to the presence of a trap, but yet close enough to discourage their drifting out of the funnel. Closer to the mouth of the corral, the stations were located increasingly close together to serve as a stronger deterrent as the animals stampeded by.

Considerable time might elapse before a herd would wander close to the fatal angle between the wings, and even then success would depend on a favorable wind blowing toward the mouth of the enclosure at the time of the hunt.

Impounding was the preferred method of capturing buffalo for slaughter in many areas on the Western Plains before the advent of horses.

Intentional firings of grass carried out in the fall of the year in carefully selected areas near the mouth of the corral resulted in a new growth of grass the next year. This lusher, greener grass was an effective stimulus to get buffalo to graze in this area.

Great restraint had to be exercised in maneuvering the herd into position between the wings. Getting the great herd moving in the proper direction was a tedious under-taking done slowly and by degrees. Initially, the animals would be prodded by a lone hunter appearing on the horizon and waving a blanket; then quickly he would duck back down out of sight. On occasion, youthful runners might have to run swiftly ahead, circumnavigating the herd in an attempt to abort a turn in the wrong direction.

Even at night, after the herd was bedded down, it was nettled closer into position by dropping a folded blanket on the ground. This dull thump caused the animals to get up, edging away from this unexpected sound, and closer to the desired position. Small smouldering fires using grass or dung were lit to encourage a leisurely drift into the wings. A strain of domesticated dogs that evolved from captured coyote and wolf pups were trained to start and control buffalo stampedes into corrals, over cliffs and into other traps. Every precaution was taken not to alarm or to prematurely stampede the herd as the welfare of the entire camp during the coming winter might well depend on a successful impoundment.

As the buffalo ambled into position between the wings and headed down the funnel toward the corral, the tempo of the drive increased. The movement of the herd reached stampede proportions, egged on by yelling and blanket-waving Indians along the narrowing path, as the edge of the impoundment was neared. By the time the lead buffalo had sensed the trap, it was already too late. In spite of sharp braking efforts, it was carried over the brink by the sheer momentum of the herd behind. Panic and confusion now blocked the buffalo's normal instincts, and this further hastened their demise. The air was so choked with dust, and the animals so tightly packed between the collapsing arms of the V, that the herd would now charge blindly into the corral.

The impoundment had to be stoutly built. The usual determining factor for the size of a corral was the number of families in the camp. Occasionally, the more moderately-sized corrals were filled to such a capacity that some of the last buffalo to enter could escape by merely clambering over the backs of their companions and on over the sides of the corral.

Once securely in the impoundment, all of the participants of the hunt triumphantly descended on the corral to perch on its edge and start killing the buffalo with bows and arrows and lances. An attempt to make the annihilation complete was made because it was feared that any escapee would warn other buffalo of the trap, and so render it useless in the future.

An added inducement for the buffalo to head in the proper direction toward the corral was achieved with a decoy by some tribes. Two Indian hunters draped hides over their bodies: one of a buffalo calf and the other of a wolf. A simulated attack on the buffalo calf by the wolf was then staged. This pantomine dramatized with bellowing, duped the buffalo into coming to the aid of the distressed calf. Such productions often were successful in coaxing the herd in the correct direction. It was essential that these human decoys were also quite fleet of foot to escape the animals' charge. In case one of the decoys was forced into the corral by the stampeding herd, a small portal was constructed for a hasty exit.

A variation of the impoundment method of slaughtering buffalo is what the Blackfeet called a "*piskin*." Literally translated, this means "deep blood kettle" and it utilized natural features of the terrain. Instead of being stampeded into a corral, the buffalo were driven over the edge of a tall cliff where they would fall to their death, or at least be so maimed that they could be easily subdued. Suitable cliffs were carefully selected and tactics for getting the herd started in the direction of the cliff, and stampeded over the edge, were essentially the same as used in the impoundment method. The women waited below the cliff out of the way of the tumbling buffalo ready with their skinning knives and *travois* for transporting the butchered carcasses back to the camp. As soon as the last buffalo plunged to his death, the women quickly moved in to club the survivors and go efficiently about their task of skinning and butchering. A few days after the drive, the stench of decaying blood and offal carried for some distance downwind. A host of scavengers ranging from eagles to coyotes to the lowly carrion beetle, moved in to clean up the remains. Only after a thorough purging by sun, wind and rain would nature, together with time restore the site for another use. The Blackfeet continued using their *piskin* long after horses were available primarily because of the older tribe members' reluctance to let tradition die. The locations of several of these buffalo jumps in the western United States are known, and the Madison Site near Butte, Montana is now a state memorial.

The foot-surround could be attempted on a windless day, and while it did not involve a wholesale slaughter as the drives did, it was an effective means of killing a few buffalo. Everyone in the camp completely encircled a small group of cows and calves to separate them from the main herd. The ring of hunters gradually closed in on the small herd, and with luck could get within thirty or forty yards (27 or 37 meters) of the nearsighted animals. When the buffalo became aware of the hunters, the animals instinctively would start milling about searching for internal protection among the herd. Capitalizing on this confusion, the Indians were afforded some easy bow and arrow shots. Eventually, the flustered herd would break through the lines and escape, but not without leaving several of their numbers behind dead or wounded.

The Ojibwa, Winnebago, Iowa and Santee Sioux of the eastern long-grass prairie effectively utilized the fire-surround. A band of hunters ignited the dry prairie grass around a herd of buffalo. The result was a ring of fire with select segments of the circle not burning. As the buffalo fled the enclosing fire through these "safe" avenues of escape, they were forced to literally run a gauntlet of armed hunters who had been stationed there to shoot the beasts as they fled.

Stalking was usually accomplished by a hunter down on all fours with a wolf skin draped over his body. This allowed an approach to within bow range of a portion of the herd. Wolves constantly prowled the fringes of buffalo herds, and while they posed a threat to an individual calf or a sick or injured adult lagging behind the main herd, healthy, mature animals scarcely paid attention to their presence. This provided just the cover the wolf skin-draped stalker needed for his approach.

Buffalo are almost constantly on the move, their wanderings necessitated by the rapidity with which they deplete the grass supply. Ambush tactics were usually foiled by the fact that these herd wanderings were totally random and completely unpredictable. Still, even on the open plains, there existed certain draws or passes that were frequently traversed by the herds. These represented nothing more than the easiest way of passing from one point to another, or perhaps they led to a scarce watering hole. The pounding of countless hooves on the ground in such places resulted in deeply worn ruts. In these furrows, a hunter smeared with mud or dust for camouflage could get a close shot at a passing buffalo by exercising patience and lying in wait.

Primitive hunters were adept at using natural barriers

or inclement conditions to hinder the mobility of a pursued animal. The Plains Indians were no exception. Expert swimmers were able to kill buffalo using a knife when they overtook them swimming wide expanses of water such as the Missouri River. The occasional winter hunting foray usually resulted when a herd was discovered wintering in a valley with deep snow. The buffalo were ungainly under such conditions and were readily subdued by snowshoe-clad hunters. Nor were sharp buffalo hooves ideally designed to gain a purchase on the slippery ice of lakes or rivers. Tribes along the Missouri, Platte, Arkansas and Kansas Rivers made a practice of herding buffalo onto the frozen rivers, surrounding them and killing the handicapped beasts. The translation of the Plains Cree term for this type of hunting was "wolf pound." Undoubtedly, the inspiration, among the Plains Cree at least, for this method of hunting was from observing packs of wolves practice the same techniques.

Hunting on Horseback

By the time of the first Anglo-American exploration of the continent west of the Mississippi by Lewis and Clark in 1805, horses were in general use among most tribes of the Western Plains. Not only did the Plains Indians possess horses, but the Lewis and Clark expedition described a sophisticated horse culture replete with trappings, methods of training, experience in breeding (the Nez Perce developed the Appaloosa strain), many legends and unparalleled expertise in riding.

The travois, used to carry buffalo meat or other supplies — even babies.

The horses that roamed the North American Continent during the Pleistocene Era had become extinct. The Plains Indians first saw horses in 1541, when Francisco Coronado, searching for the fabled Seven Cities of Cibola and their reputed vast treasures of gold, pushed north into Kansas from the Rio Grande Valley. That same year, the mounted De Soto Expedition reached the Trinity River in Texas. These Spanish Conquistadores with their horses were greeted by the Indians with fascination and no small degree of fear. They held the horses in particular awe and called them "big dogs", "elk dogs" or "mystery dogs." It was probably not, however, the horses of these early Spanish expeditions that were the ancestors of the later Plains Indian horses. The Spanish did not use mares in military excursions such as these, and hence there was no brood stock to establish a herd. Rather, the first Indian horses were probably derived from Spanish cattle ranches established along the Rio Grande River in the seventeenth century. Indians of the area were employed as cowboys and not infrequently made off with some horses, which they drove north and traded to free-ranging tribes. Also, the

Oshkosh Public Museum — Photo by Roland Reed

A group of Blackfeet move camp in search of more buffalo in Cut Bank County, Montana.

Pueblo Indians revolted against the Spanish occupation of their territory in 1680 and drove all the Spaniards out of that frontier province for twelve years. During the uprising, large herds of horses were taken by Indians and were rapidly dispersed northward through thefts and trades.

The semi-nomadic Plains tribes who had depended partly on agriculture and partly on the buffalo for subsistence were quick to realize the advantages horses offered in hunting buffalo. They soon learned that horses could outrun a buffalo in the open. It became relatively easy to cut off a few buffalo from the main herd and to kill them from horseback. The procurement of meat became not only easier but possible in any season. In unusually lean times when no meat was available, a nag pack horse might even be slaughtered to ward off starvation. The entire camp mounted on horses could now follow the meanderings of the large herds. More fresh meat could be obtained and larger stores of dried meat could be transported. The means of this new mobility, the horse, ironically became one of the very reasons for it. The grass supply for a radius of several miles about the encampment was rapidly depleted by the horses, and thus necessitated a move to new pastures.

The tipi became the ideal shelter for these increasingly nomadic people and soon totally replaced the sod covered hogans. Even the size of the tipis was affected by the use of horses. Many parts of the Plains were treeless, and tipi poles had to be carried from one campsite to the next. It was these tipi poles that formed the legs of the travois and, when only dogs were available to pull these, the tipi poles were of necessity quite short. With horse travois, longer poles could be used; the horses could pull larger and heavier hide tipi covers, and living space was proportionately expanded. Stones weighted the bases of the erected tipis to the ground, and of course these "tipi rings" of stone were left behind when camp was moved. Even today, the age of a campsite can be distinguished as dating from the pre or post-horse era by the diameter of the rings of stone.

Milwaukee Public Museum
A group of Blackfeet return to camp after a buffalo hunt — near Cut Bank, Montana.

In an amazingly short period of time, the Plains Indians underwent a metamorphosis from somewhat beggarly foot hunters to one of the premier equestrian peoples in the history of the world. Their free and adventurous lifestyle has continued to capture the imaginations and envy of more sedentary people everywhere. The primarily agricultural people in the fringe areas abandoned their lifestyles to take up the nomadic life of the buffalo culture. The Sioux forsook their rich rice-producing area of the Minnesota Lake country and moved into the Dakotas. A separate

A good buffalo horse had to be not only fast and strong but also brave enough to barge into a thundering herd, and yet intelligent enough to shy away from a wounded buffalo intent on goring.

group, the Eastern Sioux, remained behind. The Piegan, Blood and Blackfeet moved south out of Alberta, Canada into Montana. The Comanches came out of the Colorado Canyonlands onto the Southern Plains and took to horseback as full-time bison hunters. Coeur d'Alene, Nez Perce and Salish made excursions onto the high plains to supplement their salmon diet, as did the Yakima, Walla Walla and Cayuse. Though the Pawnee, Arikara and Mandan continued to grow corn, they too visited the buffalo country to hunt, whereas prior to owning horses they mostly traded for meat and hides. A universal sign language was invented to breach the communication barrier. As a result, this land of the buffalo — the Western Plains — became a melting pot of diverse Indian cultures.

A good buffalo horse had to be not only fast and strong but brave enough to barge into a thundering herd, and intelligent enough to shy away from a wounded buffalo intent on goring. An animal like this was the most highly prized possession any Plains Indian could own. The presence of such a horse within a camp could easily spell the difference between an easy life and famine. As warfare, raiding and horse-stealing became the norm among Plain tribes, constant vigilance was required in guarding a top buffalo horse.

Riding was essentially bareback with just a buffalo hide-pad strapped on the horse's back. The leather belly cinch was left loose enough that the rider could wrap his legs underneath for stability and leave his hands free to manage a weapon. Pressure with the knees and shifting of the rider's weight guided the horse. A rope of braided hair was tied to the horse's lower jaw and tucked into the rider's waistband. The halter rope was quite long, twenty-five or thirty feet (8 or 9 meters), and if the rider was thrown off he was afforded the chance of regaining his mount by catching this long rope as it trailed by.

The most common weapon used against buffalo from

horseback was the short bow. The Pawnees had a legend saying they received the bow from the moon and the sun gave them arrows. The true origin of the bow and arrow on the Western Plains is uncertain, but there is no doubt that it developed into one of the world's finest hunting instruments. Typically, Plains bows had double or recurved tips which gave a decided improvement to the cast. This shortened the working limbs to make the bow easier to use from horseback, and at the same time acted as a lever to aid in drawing. Osage orange (a member of the mulberry family) and Oregan yew were the preferred bow woods of most Plains tribes. The brushy osage orange tree, in particular, grew in river bottoms throughout most of the Western Plains. Still, in some areas, select bow wood was scarce, and smart Indian hunters were perpetually on the lookout for good pieces. They usually owned a supply of bow staves in varying phases of preparation. The raw materials, as well as finished bows, were common trade items among Plains tribes. The osage orange was difficult to work because of twists in the grain and, indeed, it may have been this characteristic that dictated that Plains bows be short. Nonetheless, the short bow, seldom exceeding 2½ feet (.8 meters) in length, proved to be the ideal weapon for the Plains hunter. And osage orange, in spite of its brushy and gnarled appearance, had superior properties of elasticity and tensile strength that far exceeded its short-comings. Considerably more power was derived from these bows by gluing green sinew strips to the backs. As the strips dried and created tension along the arc of the bow, power was greatly increased. Elk antlers, mountain sheep horns and possibly buffalo horns were also used to make bows — at least among the Shoshonis, Blackfeet, Crow and Nez Perce. It is doubtful that they offered as much in performance as they did in prestige. Certainly they were more difficult to make than wood bows. Sinew from the buffalo's loin was the favorite material for bow strings.

Serviceberry, gooseberry, cherry, and wild currant were the materials most commonly used for arrow shafts. These were cut in the late winter when the sap was running so the sticks would not split while drying. Where available, cane and certain durable reeds were also used. Fletching was obtained from the feathers of some great bird of prey such as a hawk or eagle, and it was hoped that the hunting prowess of these predators would be transferred to the arrows. Material for arrow tips varied from area to area; but bone and the tips of antler tines were used as well as several stone types including flint, chert, jasper and obsidian.

Archery practice was introduced early into child rearing. One of the first toys a young boy would be given was a tiny, but functional, bow and set of arrows. All sorts of bow and arrow games were devised. In one, a youngster shot an arrow into the ground some distance away. His companions would then shoot at this arrow and the one coming the closest was declared the winner, and this would start the next round. Most Plains youth were accomplished bow shots by early adolescence.

On the other hand, some Southern Plains tribes used lances from horseback on buffalo hunts. The practicality of this custom undoubtedly arose from a paucity of good bow wood amidst plentiful cane for lances. Unlike spears, lances were made for thrusting instead of throwing, and were not released from the grip.

Buffalo were not migratory in a seasonal manner. They were better classified as unpredictable wanderers. As astute as Plains Indians were in observing animal movements, there is no record of their having detected an established migratory pattern. Such frequent moves from one camp to another were required in the nomadic pursuit of buffalo that the tipi poles used to form the travois were worn down on their butt ends so much they had to be replaced two or three times in some years.

The Plains buffalo hunters' thorough knowledge of the

buffalo's anatomy enhanced their expertise. Broad ribs that nearly overlapped each other in the expiratory phase of respiration presented an almost impenetratable barrier to the thoracic cavity and its vital organs. A more feasible approach to the heart-lung area was behind the rib cage with the line of aim directed forward. This avenue pierced soft structures such as intestine and diaphragm on the way to the heart, lungs and great vessels.

Just as with the various drive and surround methods, considerable team effort was required for a hunt. Various organizational rules were necessary, and individual hunting efforts had to be suspended to insure a successful camp hunt. A policing unit of young braves known as dog soldiers was formed to effect these rules. The usual superstitions and ritualistic preparation that preceded most Indian hunting forays were particularly paramount to the buffalo hunt.

Scouts were forever searching for buffalo. Once a herd was located, the terrain was studied for the best approach and for the probable escape routes the buffalo would attempt. The scout then rode jubilantly into camp and announced his discovery. Older braves, familiar with the intricacies of the terrain, drew up a plan for the hunt, and, after meeting certain spiritual obligations, the men left for the chase. In a camp with many horses, the slower animals were ridden to the hunt. The fastest mounts were led so they would be fresh for the sprint into the herd.

An upwind approach to within a quarter of a mile (.4 kilometers) or closer was made. Coulees or buttes were used for concealment to get as close as possible to the grazing buffalo before the final dash. As soon as the buffalo herd sensed danger and stampeded, the horses were whipped into a gallop and could usually overtake the fleeing beasts within a half of a mile (.8 kilometers). On occasion, an approach from two directions was used to confuse the herd and to delay their attempted escape, or perhaps to cause part of the herd to run toward their pursuers.

Once the hunters caught up with the herd, the horses were urged into the fast-moving melee of dust, flying hooves and bawling beasts. Several buffalo were separated from the main body and surrounded. It was easier to control the speed and direction of this smaller group.

The buffalo horse sidled up to the flank of a buffalo and offered its rider a shot with the bow or a thrust with the lance into the posterior rib area. All the while, the horse anticipated the goring attempt that was certain to occur as soon as the buffalo perceived that it had been wounded. Sometimes, repeated arrow-shooting or lance thrusts into vital areas were required to subdue an animal. Even a small cow could be an imposing animal to kill. Mortally wounded buffalo displayed a remarkable tenacity for life, and defied the gravity of their injuries. As soon as the hunter was convinced that the buffalo had been injured to the point that it could no longer keep up with the stampede, he would spur his horse on to another quarry.

The entire chase was fraught with danger for both horse and rider. The ubiquitous prairie dog holes posed the threat of tripping the galloping horse and throwing the hunter to the ground to be pulverized by churning hooves. The only thing to do in such a situation was to grab two handfuls of belly fur on a buffalo passing overhead and hang on until dragged clear of the thundering fracas.

Young calves in the herd frequently could not keep up with the fleet-footed adults and would tire quickly. Exhausted, they would hide in the tall prairie grass. Young boys, not yet old enough for the main hunt, would follow along and sharpen their hunting skills on these hapless, trembling animals.

The chase would end quickly: either when enough buffalo had been dropped or, more frequently, when the mount was so winded that urging it on was likely to result in its stumbling from exhaustion. The mounts were checked and slowly walked back across the massacre site. Their nostrils would flare and their sides heave in an attempt to regain their wind. Slathers of sweaty foam would drip from their necks and flanks. Buffalo carcasses lay strewn across the prairie. Though feathered with arrows and mortally wounded, many buffalo still had a breath of life remaining. They would arch their backs and bristle when the hunters approached, and then fall to the ground from loss of blood. These bleary-eyed beasts were finished off by the less successful participants of the hunt. Not infrequently, there were also moans from braves with broken limbs, concussions and other injuries. Horses too, were often killed in the chase.

The hunters, euphoric from the excitement of the chase, tallied their kills, swapped tales and boasted of their bravery. The women, who had been hiding downwind, came forth to start their task of skinning and butchering. Excitedly, they would scurry about among the fallen carcasses looking for those containing their husbands' arrows. From these, they would be entitled to the choice parts, but were expected to share the remainder with widows, the elderly and with the families of less fortunate hunters.

The cuts of meat from butchered buffalo were wrapped in the green hides, and this bundle was lashed onto a *travois* for transport to camp. If camp was some distance away, and if the hunt was quite successful, the tipis might be taken down and moved to the kill site. If this was the case, or if so many animals had been slain that not all of the meat and hides could be brought into camp before nightfall, a sentinel was posted with each remaining carcass. Women and children tended small fires, and when wolves, coyotes or other predators lurked too close to the slain buffalo, they would toss a tuft of dried grass on the fire to cause a short burst of flame. This was usually sufficient to drive away hungry prowlers — at least for a while. As the scene of activity shifted back to camp, the scant remains of buffalo left by the Indians were claimed by scavengers. The carnivores just below man on the food chain, the wolves, foxes and coyotes, were the first to feast on the remains. Their quarrels and fights were heard through the night. At first light, the diurnal members of the clean-up crew, such as eagles and ravens, completed the task. There was no waste of nature's bounty.

Meanwhile in the Indian camp, night overtook the operation as the last loads were dumped on the growing mounds of fresh meat beside each tipi. An orange glow from many fires encompassed the camp. Choice cuts of meat were roasted over open fires. Dogs, tied up so they couldn't raid the meat piles, were tossed some less-than-prime cuts to quiet their howling. Children, their faces smeared with grease, sucked the congealed marrow out of long bones that had been roasted over hot embers. Men laughed, sang, danced and bragged while waiting for a calf's head to bake buried in the ground under a pile of hot coals. It had been a good day this time, and it was a time of merriment. There was plenty to eat. The buffalo hunt had been a success.

It is probably true that no single animal ever exerted a

stronger influence on human culture than did the buffalo on the Indians of the Western Plains. Buffalo numbers were greatly decimated after the white man came to the Plains. The introduction of firearms was not so much the culprit as was the desire for hides. Buffalo-hide overcoats were both practical and fashionable, and many thousands of the durable hides were tanned and made into machine belting for the mills of industrial New England and Europe. The hide trade resulted in rampant killing and waste by whites and Indians alike. Hide-stripped carcasses were left to rot, and Indians depended on trade staples as the mainstay of their diet and to fulfill most of their needs. Certainly, white traders encouraged these actions. Yet, in retrospect, it seems likely that the ultimate fate of the buffalo was sealed when horses were first obtained by Plains Indians. Agricultural practices, becoming more prevalent and increasingly complex and productive, were suddenly abandoned for an easier and more glamorous lifestyle. A highly efficient harvesting method was pitted against a resource that was renewable, but which nonetheless, started showing signs of giving out before the final years of slaughter began. Enormous quantities of buffalo were killed by mounted hunters to feed a rapidly increasing Plains population who were almost totally dependent on this single animal for their existence. Increased affluence also led to increased waste. With this situation, the die was cast. The hide trade served only to hasten the buffalo's inevitable demise.

Hunting other Game

The significance of all other game hunted by Plains Indians pales when compared to the buffalo. Antelope were probably next in importance. Certainly, they were next in abundance, and indeed probably even exceeded buffalo in total numbers. Being a small animal of less contrasting coloration, and banding in small groups instead of vast herds, they received less attention from the early chroniclers than did the buffalo, and they could not be overtaken by horse-mounted hunters. A mature buck would not exceed seventy or eighty pounds (32 or 36 kilograms) and did not provide much meat for the effort expended in slaughtering one. Furthermore, their hide tanned poorly and made inferior leather.

Since antelope were not adaptable to horseback hunting, the brush corral method of harvesting persisted well into the post contact era. A herd of animals was

The antelope's curiosity was used against it in this commonly employed method of hunting.

Pronghorn antelope, mountain goat
and big horn sheep also shared the
plains and foothills and were hunted.

Sharptail grouse

Canada geese

Wolf

Sage grouse

stampeded into flimsy corrals made of piled-up sagebrush with a funnel at the entrance, not dissimilar in configuration to those used for buffalo. Such agile animals could have easily vaulted these enclosures, but some quirk of their nature prevented them from doing so.

The antelope's innate curiosity made them easy prey for a hunter hiding just below the skyline of a ridge, waving some eagle feathers on a stick so they could be seen by a herd in the valley below. Their insatiable curiosity, piqued by this unfamiliar object waving in the breeze, prompted them to walk to within easy ambush range. White plainsmen were taught this method of hunting by the Indians and called it "tolling for antelope."

Rocky mountain bighorn sheep have not always been the timid dwellers of high and remote places they are today. Prior to the encroachment of white civilization, they frequented bluffs along the Yellowstone and Little Missouri Rivers and inhabited the Black Hills as recently as 1860. They were not only plentiful, but probably the easiest of all hooved game to stalk and kill with a bow and arrow. The Shoshoni were adept at luring sheep into close bow range during the rut by clashing stones together to simulate the sound of rams battering their horns during a supremacy fight.

The Cheyenne, Blackfeet and Arapahoes all set nooses in timbered areas to catch elk in a manner identical to the method used by Athapaskan tribes in Canada for caribou.

The grizzly bear elicited well deserved respect from Plains Indians and was seldom hunted before firearms were available.

Rabbits and prairie dogs made challenging targets for aspiring young buffalo hunters. A more effective method for waylaying prairie dogs was to plug their burrow exits with manure or grass and then dig a basin around the hole. This basin was filled with water, and when the plug was removed a torrent of water rushed into the hole. This rapidly evicted the soaked occupants, who were clubbed by a waiting hunter as they emerged.

The Western Plains were rife with prairie chickens. The famous chronicler of western Indian life, George Catlin, described in his journals (1832-1839) how grass fires were used to harvest these fowl. The prairie chickens, capable of only short, sporadic flights, kept flying ahead of the advancing fire and landing until the flames again caught up with them. When a draw containing some trees was encountered, the birds would alight in the branches hoping, at this height, to gain a longer reprieve from the fire. Hunters, armed with bows and arrows, capitalized on this by hiding in camouflage among the trees and shooting the prairie chickens as they arrived. Catlin did not state if the fires were from natural causes or if they were intentionally set.

Part of the Western Plains is within the central flyway, and is visited seasonally by tens of thousands of migrating ducks and geese. As they made brief rest stops on the prairie potholes during their flight, they were too tempting for Plains Indian hunters to ignore. It was while noting how

Sinew-wrapped bundles of rushes were made to closely resemble canvasback ducks and used as decoys.

Birds of prey were captured by hunters lying in wait in a concealed pit that was baited.

these wary waterfowl trustingly splashed down among their own kind on a lake that the idea of a duck decoy was born. Excavations of Lovelock Cave in Nevada's Humboldt Range in 1924 yielded almost a dozen decoys made of bulrushes: woven, shaped and tied to realistically resemble canvasback ducks. Long white feathers were inserted along the sides to copy the male's flanks, and black and rust pigments were used to color the head and back. These decoys were set at the edge of reeds in open water while the hunter hid in vegetation closer to shore. His black hair sprinkled with cattail pollen to blend better with his surroundings, the Indian hunter would dabble his fingers in the water to mimic the sound of feeding waterfowl.

Among common items of barter, only horses exceeded eagle feathers in trade value. Feathers were used for personal adornment and were symbolic of wealth and accomplishment for the owner. Eagles and hawks were caught by hand. A pit large enough to conceal a hunter was dug. While the hunter crouched in the pit, his companion covered the top with a lattice-work of brush, and baited the trap with a dead rabbit. The concealed hunter had only to wait until some bird of prey was attracted to the bait. He then sprang through the brush covering and grabbed the unsuspecting bird by the legs.

The buffalo culture was doomed by the introduction of horses. The culture flickered for a brief two-hundred years. Like the sea-faring Vikings and the knights of King Arthur, the Plains Indians life style has excited the imaginations of men ever since. What would the Lewis and Clark Expedition have found if horses had never been re-introduced into the New World? There would have probably existed a culture of sedentary people practicing agriculture and exhibiting decreasing dependency on hunting as a way of providing. History would have been robbed of one of its most colorful chapters.

Sea lions David Hancock

Hunters of the Sea

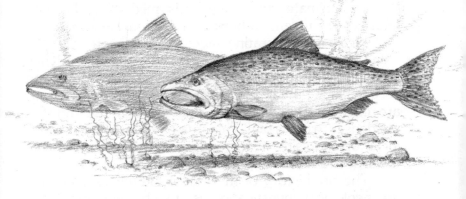

Salmon virtually hurl themselves on the doorstep of Northwest Coast peoples and make bountiful catches a predictable annual event.

The Pacific Northwest Coast is a narrow 1,400 mile (2,253 kilometer) strip of land extending from Cape Mendocino in northern California, along the coasts of Oregon, Washington and British Columbia to Prince William Sound in Southeast Alaska. The area is buttressed by the Coastal Mountains to the east and hammered by the vast Pacific Ocean on the west. The longest stretch of open ocean in the Northern Hemisphere, 6,000 miles (9,656 kilometers) from Japan, gathers its forces and unleashes them relentlessly on the beach creating a dynamic meeting of earth and sea. There are numerous offshore islands and narrow, deep, fjord-like inlets. The land is drenched with a rainfall that averages 115 inches (292 centimetres) per year in some areas. The frequently mist-shrouded shoreline is punctuated with several great rivers that bring this moisture back to whence it came — the sea. Rivers of the south are the Squamish, the Fraser and the venerable Columbia. The central portion has its Nimpkish and Bella

Coola Rivers and there are the Stikine, the Nass and the Skeena Rivers to the north.

The climate, though wet, is mild. The Japanese (Kuroshio) Current bathes the entire coast in warm water and exerts its moderating effect on the climate. Moisture rising from these warm ocean currents travels inland where it hits the vertical Coastal Mountains. As the water vapor ascends along the face of this range, cooler temperatures are encountered at higher altitudes and the moisture condenses to fall as rain. This creates a veritable rain forest, ideal for exquisite stands of spruce, fir, cedar, yew and, towards the southern portions, redwood.

The pre-history of the area is sketchy at best, and archaeological investigation is fraught with difficulties. Pottery and flaked stone tools were not utilized by the Indians of this area, and these reliable clues to the past are mostly absent from Northwest Coast excavations. The material most used to make weapons, tools, and containers in this region was, inevitably, wood, which is perishable. Also, it is quite natural that a people inhabiting this coast line would feast on the abundant clams and shells. Vast quantities of this shell debris, representing many years accumulation, further hamper investigations. Some fortunate exceptions to many of these difficulties exist at the Ozette Site on Washington's coast. On a rainy night about 500 years ago, an avalanche of mud cascaded down the side of a mountain and covered the Makah Indian village that lay at its base. The thick ooze sealed the town and its sleeping inhabitants in an air-tight tomb. Washington State University's excavation of this site has produced thousands of well-preserved artifacts. The fruit of this disaster has been a wealth of information about the people of the Northwest Coast and the lives they led.

Contact between the white man and natives of the Northwest Coast was first made by Russian explorers in the Eighteenth Century. The earliest documented visit was in 1741 by Captain Alexi Cherikov who was sailing in a sister ship with Vitus Bering, a Dane exploring for the Russian crown. The ships of Cherikov and Bering became separated in heavy fog and rain. Bering's ship sailed northward where he discovered Bering Straits. The original intent of the voyage was to determine if there was a land bridge between the Kamchatka Peninsula on the tip of Siberia and North America. Meanwhile, Cherikov, in the second ship, drifted toward Southeast Alaska. He had only fleeting glimpses of some Tlingits in canoes around the area of Chichagof Island. Cherikov had lost both of his shore-landing craft in earlier exploration attempts and was not able to establish contact with these people. This was not terribly disappointing to him as he was convinced that he was amidst hostile savages and was anxious to depart for the homeland and report to the Czar.

Things were not going as planned for Bering either. He became ill and his ship was wrecked on an island. Though his scurvy-ridden crew was able to make repairs and return to Siberia, Bering died. While repairing their ship, Bering's crew survived by eating the flesh of sea otters, which were in abundance on the island. A few sleek otter pelts were taken back home where they awed the Russians and started the quest for furs in the Pacific Northwest.

Russian fur traders, the *promyshleniki*, plied these coastal waters for the next half century and developed a close contact with natives of the area. The culture they encountered was perhaps the most sophisticated in North America. No beggarly primitives living a meager existence were these people. Nor were they dazzled by the glass beads, cloth, metal goods and other trinkets brought to their shores by fur traders. They realized the value of their own resources and were a people concerned with wealth, status and material possessions. An extensive trade network up and down the coast existed prior to white contact. In the north, trade routes extended inland to the Athapaskans; to the south goods were bartered with Plateau and even Plains tribes by the coast dwellers. This resulted in considerable trading expertise in dealing with the fur traders.

Rather than in tribes, the Northwest Coast Indians lived in villages, several of which comprised a regional group. In the north, from Icy Bay down the panhandle of Southeast Alaska, lived the Tlingits. Those skilled woodworkers and carvers of argillite stone, the Haida, lived on the Queen Charlotte Islands. The shore and coastal islands of British Columbia were inhabited by the Tsimshians, Bella Coolas, and Kwakiutls. The west shore of Vancouver Island belonged to the seafaring Nootkas, and the coasts of Washington, Oregon, and northern California were home for several groups of coastal Salish.

These people exhibited a precisely determined hierarchal social structure with revered village chiefs at the top. Slaves, obtained through trade, occupied the bottom rung. Villages consisted of several moieties or clans, each adapting its own special emblematic animal such as the eagle, raven or whale. Members of a clan would all live in a large wooden house 30 feet (9 meters) or more wide and up to 100 feet (30 meters) long. These were constructed of overlapping red cedar planks lashed to a frame with rope woven from inner bark of the cedar tree. A fire pit occupied the center of the house; sleeping benches, covered with cedar bark mats, were arranged around the periphery. Social status determined living space within the house with the upper hierarchy in the center near the fire. Several of these houses, all facing the sea, made up a village.

Fierce pride within a clan, and the intense rivalry that resulted between different clans, were the source of one of the most bizarre social customs ever recorded. The potlatch was a lavish ceremony lasting for several days. It was the culmination of perhaps a year of preparation. This was a feast given by an individual, with the help of his fellow clan members, to impress the members of another clan with wealth, status, and prestige. During the celebration, gifts would be bestowed upon the guests, the value of each carefully matched to the social status of the recipient. Potlatches served as an investment in the future as generosity was expected to be reciprocated at a future ceremony — with interest accrued. Each potlatch became progressively more elaborate in an attempt to outdo previous ones. Well-rehearsed dances and performances were given by guests and hosts alike. Feasting bordered on gorging. Among the most affluent, wealth was often destroyed rather than given away, just to awe the guests. The performers threw precious seal oil on the fire and cut up Chilcat blankets which had been laboriously woven from mountain goat hair and cedar bark. Sometimes, they even killed a slave for the benefit of their visitors. Occasionally, the corpses of slain slaves were placed on the beach with their hands and feet bound, and served as rollers to aid in beaching the canoes of dignitaries attending the potlatch. In a subliminal way, this contest of wealth may have prevented war-like hostilities. Outwardly, it was a method used to gain acceptance, prestige, and social eminence.

The art that emblazoned the natives' house fronts, totem poles, storage containers, and canoe prows was highly developed, symbolic, and usually portrayed in abstract design the animal that represented a clan or lineage. It was a bold, stylized art form that is probably the most distinctive of any primitive culture.

The drab everyday clothing of these people was not in concert with other highly decorative aspects of their culture, though it was ideally suited to this raincoast. Women scantily clad themselves in short skirts or kilts, and men dressed in breech cloths woven from the inner bark of the cedar tree or from mountain goat hair. Leather did not retain heat when wet and dried slowly; furthermore, it hardened and became brittle after repeated dousings and so was not practical in such a wet climate.

The Indians went barefoot as people must who are constantly stepping in and out of water.

The bold, stylized art form of the Northwest Coast culture was immediately apparent in their villages on house fronts, totem poles and canoe prows.

It is a general axiom of cultural anthropology that the development and sophistication of a people is inversely proportional to the degree of struggle required for day-to-day survival. The great material wealth and elaborate social structure of the Northwest Coast bespeaks of a people who lived amidst abundance. Normally, such an easy lifestyle is associated with fertile land and advanced agricultural practices. The people of the Northwest Coast practiced no agriculture. Rather, they were children of the sea. Their life was dominated by a benevolent ocean that teemed with life. The beaches had an opulence of shellfish. Cod and halibut were plentiful beyond the offshore kelp beds. Smelt and herring swarmed through the surf. Huge sturgeon swam along deep river bottoms.

And then there were salmon. Some mysterious force compelled these fish to climb coastal rivers in their quest for ancestral spawning gravel. The life cycle of the salmon made bountiful catches a predictable annual event. Only a few months, roughly May through September, were required for obtaining provisions for the year, as well as a surplus for trade. This left ample time for honing artistic skills, for developing a complex and advanced society, and for enjoying the amenities of life.

Salmon Fishing

There are five species of salmon inhabiting the waters of the Pacific Northwest: the chinook or king, the coho or silver, the chum or dog, the pink or humpback, and the sockeye. Salmon are what fish biologists call anadromous; they live in both fresh and salt water. Adult salmon spend three or four years cruising the open seas. Here fertile waters enable rapid growth until some internal biological clock sends these fish in a search for the river of their birth.

The salmon may mill about the estuary of their river until water conditions are right for an ascent, and then one of the most amazing rituals of propagation in nature begins. Obsessed with the need to deposit and fertilize eggs over the same river bottom where they were born, the salmon are undaunted by long miles, raging currents, steep waterfalls and predators to obtain their objective. It is a rendezvous with death because the fish that do not succumb to the perilous journey will die anyway after spawning. The struggle up each stretch of rapids, every jump over the many falls, takes an increasing toll on the bodies of the salmon until they are close to death. After futile attempts at especially torrential sections where the fish are swept back by the current onto their sides in the increasingly shallow river, they will right themselves and try again. Their snouts are rubbed raw, their fins and tails are mere bony stubs, and blotches of gray fungus cause slabs of skin to peel off their bodies. Still, as the desired stretch of river is reached, strength is somehow mustered for the climax of the struggle. Writhing in their final agonies, the female deposits her eggs over roughly prepared nests (redd) in the stream bottom, and the male, swimming at her side, fertilizes these eggs. The goal of this arduous journey will be achieved by at least a few salmon.

Just as the act of spawning assures life, it is followed by death. Too emaciated to resist the current any longer, the salmon are swept downstream. They will soon join their hatchmates, paled skeletons strewn over the river bottom and about the banks to become food for scavengers and predators.

The eggs, at least the ones that escape insect predation, hatch the following spring. These youngsters are called alevin and have a pendulous yolk sac attached to their ventral surface. They derive nourishment from this yolk sac until they are mature enough to forage for themselves. These young salmon or parr spend their first year in the freshwater river. The parr's existence is tenuous. They must escape the heron who stalk the shallows, aerial attacks from kingfishers and ospreys, and threats from diving mergansers. This is to say nothing of the mink and otters who also relish fish. The parr descend to the sea in their second year and may live more than a thousand miles from the river to which they must someday return.

Parr do not resemble mature salmon in size or coloration, and apparently the Northwest Coast dwellers never associated the two. The Tlingits, Kwakiutls, and others believed that salmon were a race of non-mortal men who lived in houses beneath the sea through the winter. Each spring these people transformed into salmon and swarmed into the rivers for the purpose of feeding the land-dwelling humans. After their flesh had been devoured, it was important that all of the bones be tossed back into the river or sea to be reborn. Failure to do so might result in the crippling of one of the salmon people, or, worse yet, cause them not to return the next year. Even though the abundance of salmon was explained on a supernatural basis, the Nootka may have been responsible for the first fish-stocking program in America. They transported salmon eggs from one stream to another to create a salmon run in a stream that had none, or only a small migration.

The first salmon caught at the start of the run each year was accorded all the honors of a high-ranking visitor. This particular fish was taken to a specially designated person who performed a ceremonial welcome. He placed the fish on an altar with its head pointing upstream to show the rest of the fish the direction to swim and sprinkled the salmon with eagle down. He then cooked the fish and everyone in the village partook of the flesh. Only after the bones were properly returned to the sea could the village men begin fishing.

In the salmon's drive to reach the spawning grounds,

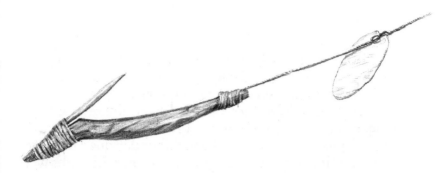

Salmon were caught at sea and in river estuaries by trolling a wooden-shanked hook with a bone or copper barb lashed on with spruce root. An abalone shell enticer enhanced its effectiveness.

they were imperiled by numerous obstacles placed in their path by the Northwest Coast people. Through well-planned alterations along select sections of the migration route and by the employment of some ingenious devices, the salmon's river gauntlet became a prolific food source for the coastal Indians.

After entering the river, salmon hardly fed at all so weirs, traps, nets, and spears had to be used to catch the fish here. But at sea, and while congregated in river estuaries, they could be caught on hook and line by trolling, using a straight-shanked composite hook. The shanks were usually fashioned from wood, sometimes ivory, and the barb was a sharp spicule of bone or copper. The shank and barb were lashed together with spruce root. It was necessary for the leader to be quite fine in diameter so as to be nearly invisible to the salmon. Materials used included doe skin, braided human hair, whale baleen, and twine made from cedar bark or nettle fiber. The Indians baited the hook with tom cod, shiner or herring tied to the barb. Sometimes the leader was graced with an abalone shell flasher or exciter. This rig was trolled from a canoe on a handline. A couple of turns of the line were made around the paddle. This caused the bait to jerk enticingly as the boat was paddled and also ensured an instant set when the fish struck.

Both fish spears and harpoons were designed to hook as well as to pierce, and each could have single or multiple prongs. There the similarities ended. While harpoons were thrown, spears were not released from the grip and had longer handles for an extended reach. Spear heads were fixed in place, but harpoon heads were designed to detach from the shaft once contact was made, and the barbs were fixed in the flesh. The harpoon head was attached to its shaft with a braided line. The tips of the harpoon heads were made of bone, slate, mussel shell, and, of course, later, iron. Each of these materials could be made razor-sharp. The bi-valved barbs were fashioned from split tips of deer or elk antler tines.

Waiting for salmon to enter the mouth of a river, a Nootka poises his harpoon in readiness.

A Wishham fisherman catches a salmon with his double-pronged spear along the Columbia River.

The coastal dwellers used spears within the confines of a weir or trap. In some of the deeper sections of rivers, however, and particularly at the mouths, freeswimming salmon were harpooned. Channels were cleared through the beds of kelp that grew on shallow bars in the river estuaries. The course of such channels was selected with an eye towards proper water depth and clarity for good harpooning. Salmon naturally followed these cleared paths into the rivers. In this manner they were manipulated into position of advantage for harpooners who tied their boats up over these channels and waited. Crushed clam shells were spread over the bottom, and the light reflected from their pearled surface highlighted fish that swam through, making them easier to see.

Tidal fluctuations were effectively utilized to catch great numbers of salmon. Amassed at river mouths and

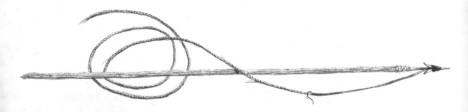

A typical Northwest Coast harpoon with line fastened to the detachable head.

along beaches before ascending to their spawning grounds, the milling salmon rode the tidal drift as the tides ebbed and flowed. Great semicircular stone fences were constructed well below the high tide line. During the high tide, the unsuspecting salmon lolled with the flow over the top of the trap. As the tide ebbed, the top of the stone fence stuck up above the water, and prevented the fish from returning to the sea. Remains of these stone traps are still evident at several places along the Northwest Coast. A variation of the tidal trap was a crib made of poles driven into the bottom with a lattice of sticks woven through them. The opening of the crib faced the land, and fence weirs extended from this opening to funnel salmon into the trap as the tide receded.

Salmon weir on the Cowichan River. British Columbia Provincial Museum, Victoria

Semicircular stone weirs were constructed to take advantage of fluctuations of tides to entrap fish.

The sinuous rivers with their deep gorges, rocky ledges, midstream boulders, shallow rapids, and waterfalls presented the Indians with as many opportunities as they did the salmon with obstacles. Rivers were diligently studied to determine which particular mode of fishing, or what trap structure could best serve the Indians' purpose.

Available building materials and cultural background also influenced the type of trap constructed. Each of these devices reflected a keen understanding of the river and its life by the Indians. The best fishing locations were owned by villages, clans or families; this constituted one of the few instances of property ownership rights among primitive peoples. In some cases, these were handed down from one generation to the next, or gained through marriage. Smaller tributary streams or less productive sections of the river were sometimes made available to individuals for fishing, though ownership rights varied among different bands. Many of the largest traps were projects of an entire village and all shared in the construction, the manning, and in the catching. As the salmon progressed upstream, their condition deteriorated and their numbers were depleted. Villages near the mouth of the river would jeer bands living further upstream for the soft-fleshed, nearly dead fish that they caught and ate. Still, they customarily allowed enough fish to pass through their traps so that these inland cultures could survive. This gesture may have been more from fear of retaliation than from kindness of heart; their traps and weirs could be easily sabotaged by a huge log sent cascading downstream.

Interior Salish salmon weir, platform and dip net.

Weirs were used to concentrate spawning salmon so they could be easily dip netted.

Weirs were essentially fences through which water flowed. The support pilings driven into the river bottom for some of these structures were a permanent fixture, and the lattice work would be added just before each run. The weirs could be utilized in two ways: by diverting migrating salmon into some type of trap, or by concentrating the fish in a

Leisters and spears were used at traps and weirs.

narrow, shallow area where they could be speared or dip netted.

Several configurations of multiple-pronged spears were adapted to this type of fishing. One three-prong style of spear carried points on only the outer prongs while the tipless center prong was left a few inches longer. This protected the fragile points on the outer prongs if the fish was missed and the bottom struck. The leister, another three-pronged spear, had a sharp center prong to impale the fish and outer prongs made of some springy substance such as whale baleen or green wood. These outer prongs carried barbs that would hold the fish firmly on the center prong. Gaff hooks made of bone or antler and hafted to a long handle were used at weirs. A quick raking motion with the gaff over the backs of the fish was successful in impaling them.

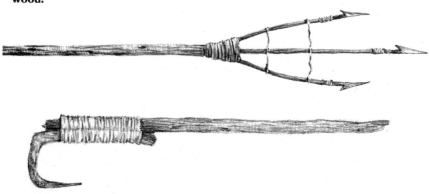

A leister typically had a sharp center prong to impale the fish and outer prongs made of some springy substance such as whale baleen or green wood.

Gaff hooks were commonly used where fish were concentrated at weirs.

A Hupa Indian waits for salmon with his multiple-pronged spear.

Various sizes of conical and cylindrical basket traps were designed to be used in conjunction with weirs. These were typically made of hemlock bough hoops and split cedar ribs. Once within the confines of a conical basket trap, the salmon, in their eagerness to swim up stream, would keep wedging themselves tighter into the small end. The smaller models were just large enough for a single fish, and there was no room inside for the fish to turn around. These were used in the shallow, swift portions of small feeder streams. In the larger basket traps used with weirs, it was the relatively small exit portal that the salmon were unable to locate.

Conical basket traps were used in shallow sections of the river.

Basket traps were also used in conjunction with weirs.

A particularly clever and effective trap that was extensively used by the Nootkas was built at the base of a waterfall. A pole framework supported a slanted shelf and backstop of lattice work. The lip of the shelf was positioned close enough to the waterfall to interfere slightly with the salmon's jump. Unable to reach the crest of the falls, the salmon would tumble back onto the slanted shelf and could not flop back into the river.

As might be expected of an existence based on fishing, the Northwest Coast culture exhibited considerable sophistication in the making of cordage and in the weaving of nets. Nettle plants, those tormenting stingers of bare skin, grow tall along the raincoast. This plant was the source of the best cordage for netting. The stalks were cut, split, dried and then beaten so the fiber could be teased apart. This fiber was then spun into twine using either a spindle or by rolling the fiber between the palm and thigh. Willow bark and inner cedar bark (the cambium layer) were also used for nets.

Gill nets were set across rivers. When salmon ran into these barriers, their gill covers got caught in the mesh. The more the salmon struggled to free themselves, the more they became entangled. Long seines were effectively used along protected beaches and in estuaries where salmon congregated. Large bag nets with their bottom corners weighted could be dragged between two canoes in quiet river eddies. These nets were equipped with ivory or horn rings so the mouth could be closed in purse string fashion before being hauled up. Large nets with their corners weighted were placed on the bottom in those channels cleared through the kelp beds where harpooning was done. Two canoes were stationed, one along each side of the net. When the salmon were spotted swimming over the net in the clear water, the Indians quickly raised the net by its lines. As it was hauled up, the two canoes swung close together. The net was pulled into one canoe while the salmon dropped into the other.

In some rivers the torrential rush of water was too great to erect any type of trap or weir. The Klickitat, a tributary of the Columbia, was such a river. It thundered through a steep, rocky gorge. The roar of the rapids was deafening. Gulls and eagles flew unsteadily in the turbulent

230

Fall traps were positioned at the base of a waterfall in just such a manner as to interfere with the salmon's leap so that it would fall back helplessly onto the lattice work of the structure.

A Hupa Indian uses a V-shaped dip net from a platform above the Trinity River.

air currents that swept through the gorge. In many places there was no bank. Salish tribes along this river rigged fragile-appearing platforms over the thundering water. Laboriously suspended from the cliff wall by lines and poles, the station was constantly enshrouded in mist that rose from the turbulent river. From precarious perches such as these, Indians dip-netted salmon. These large dip-nets were suspended from a V-shaped frame, and the mesh was quite large so as to offer less resistance against the water's thrust.

Denver Public Library — Western History Department — Photo by Edward Curtis
Dip-netting salmon from a platform — Wishham.

Salmon were roasted on spits over open fires, cooked by the stone-boiling method in watertight bentwood boxes, and steamed in pits lined with hot rocks, wet leaves and seaweed. These were methods of cooking fresh fish. All the riches of the sea and rivers would have been wasted were it not for the ability to preserve the catch for future use.

Along southern portions of the coast where there was less moisture and warm, dry winds were a bit more predictable, salmon were filleted and cut in strips to be preserved through the dehydrating effect of wind and sun. Racks were situated high on rocky outcrops to capture the greatest drying effect. Along most of the coastal area with its greater dampness, there may have been some drying of fish, but most of the preservation was accomplished by smoking. Cedar-planked smoke houses were built in all the villages. Strips and fillets of salmon were even hung from the rafters of dwellings. A fire constantly burned in the central pit with its smoke spiraling up through the suspended racks of salmon. Skewers of salmon heads were dried and smoked as well because the masseter muscle of the cheek was considered a delicacy. Tails, with a center strip of meat containing the backbone, were dried over a fire until crisp, and then stored in boxes for snacks.

The Nootka and the Haida were island dwellers and were not blessed with salmon rivers the way coastal inhabitants were. They were forced into a greater dependence upon the open sea for their existence. The Makah of the Olympic Peninsula were also great ocean fishermen. The canoes of these seafarers were master-pieces in cedar with their graceful lines and high prows. They were marvelously seaworthy. Fashioned from a single cedar log using fire and adze as were dugouts, these canoes in no way resembled the crude dugouts. Red cedar, straight-grained and relatively soft, was perhaps the only wood that could be worked so well with primitive adzes, mauls and hardwood wedges. The Haida made the finest vessels, and some ceremonial models measured up to 60 feet (18.5 meters) in length with ornately carved prows. Other groups recognized the expertise of the Haida as canoe carvers, and these canoes became important trade items. There were several lengths, styles, and keel forma-tions depending on their intended use. Some were designed for stability on the ocean and others for maneuverability on rivers. The rough canoe forms were expertly shaped with the adze and then a minimum hull thickness was obtained by using the abrasive, sandpaper-like skin of the dogshark.

Halibut Fishing

Inhabiting the shallow waters of the continental shelf is a surrealistic-appearing denizen: the halibut. Although it did not differ greatly at one time in evolutionary terms from the usual preconception of a fish, the halibut adapted to an existence on the floor of the ocean. Evolutionary changes included a total shift of body axis from vertical to horizontal and a migration of the left eye to the top of the head. The fish averaged 30 pounds (14 kilograms) in weight and frequently exceeded 200 pounds (91 kilograms). The halibut was the species that most bottom-fishing efforts were directed toward.

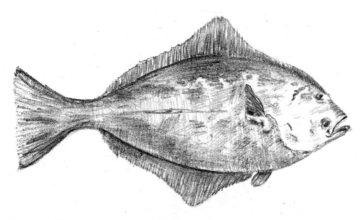

Halibut are bizarre-appearing off-shore denizens that were eagerly harvested by Northwest Coast people.

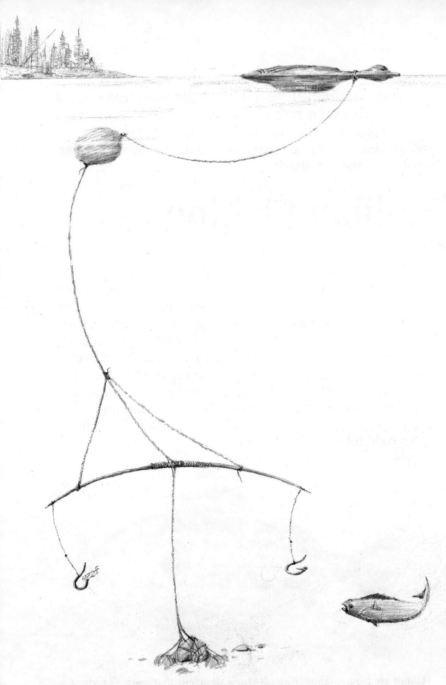

Steam-bent hooks were fished just off the bottom in pairs separated by a spreader bar. They were usually baited with octopus.

Two distinctively different styles of hooks were used for halibut. Both were apparently equally effective, but cultural mores dictated the use of each style in a particular area. The horseshoe size steam-bent hook was the one used in central and southern portions of the coast. Sticks were whittled to the proper length and thickness from spruce, fir or yew. Only wood from knots or the lower portions of tree trunks were dense enough to prevent the hook from floating in the water. (Density of wood decreases progressively from the trunk to the tree's upper reaches.) These sticks were then inserted with water into containers fashioned from the bulbous end floats of the kelp plant. Stoppered with moss, these were placed over hot embers for steaming. The sticks, easily bent after being steamed, were placed in a mold that was carved in a slab of wood. After cooling, the wood retained the desired shape. Bone barbs were attached by spruce root.

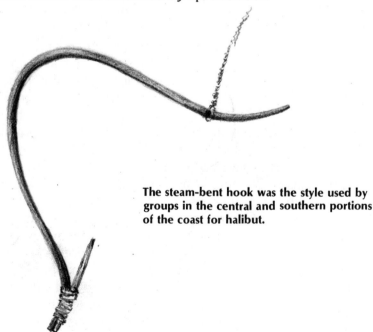

The steam-bent hook was the style used by groups in the central and southern portions of the coast for halibut.

Slices of octopus or devil fish were lashed with nettle fiber to the throat of the hook just beneath the barb. The barb itself was not covered. The large outer bend of the hook forced the fish to put its mouth over the barb when it approached the bait. These rigs were fished just off the bottom in pairs separated by a spreader bar. A grooved stone served as a sinker and an inflated seal's bladder suspended the baited hooks about a yard from the ocean floor. The main line was made of kelp which grows on rocky shelves off the Pacific Northwest Coast. With one end of the plant tenaciously attached to the bottom, the other end terminated in a bulb that floated on the surface. Often 100 feet (30 meters) in length, kelp could be soaked in fresh water, dried, and joined by a special knot into long, stout fishing lines capable of enduring considerable use. Wooden marker buoys, tied to the surface end of the kelp line, marked the rig's location. These were often carved in the artistic forms of birds, fish or sea otters. Their elliptical shape permitted them to float upright when the weight of a fish was on the line. Fishermen observing several floats from a nearby canoe were alerted to a catch in this manner.

In the post-contact era, hemp line replaced spruce root, rope replaced kelp, and iron was used for barbs instead of bone. That the basic design of the steam-bent hook was not altered with these improvements attests to its effectiveness.

To the north, the Tlingit, the Haida, and the Tsimshian used the classic 2-piece, V-shaped halibut hook. The arm opposite the barb was usually ornately carved into a spiritual helper. Otters, seals, halibut, wolves and an assortment of sea monsters were the customary motifs. Like the steam-bent hook, they were fished about a yard off the bottom but usually singly instead of in pairs. The northern style halibut hook with a bone barb had sufficient buoyancy to float at the desired height above its sinker. Rocks served as sinkers and were attached to the line with

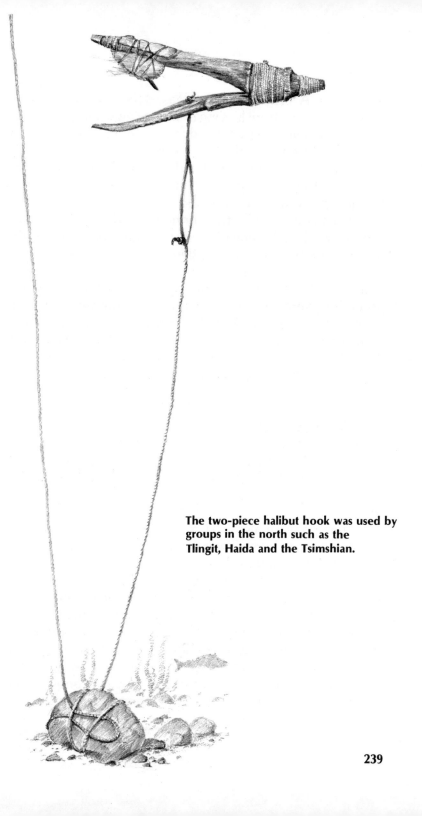

The two-piece halibut hook was used by groups in the north such as the Tlingit, Haida and the Tsimshian.

a slip knot. A jerk of the line released this knot, and left the weight on the bottom leaving only line separating the angler from his fish Iron barbs, used after contact with the white man, interfered with the natural buoyancy of the rig and required a float tied just ahead of the hook. The design carved on these wooden floats often complemented that on the decorated arm of the hook.

These hooks, with their bone-barbed arms floating on top, were ideally engineered for the anatomy of the halibut's mouth. With a sudden flaring of the operculum, or gill covers, the halibut creates a vacuum within its mouth, and water and food are sucked in. It can reverse the procedure and expel food by forcefully compressing its gill covers. After taking the baited portion of a hook into its mouth and realizing that it could not swallow this morsel, the halibut would try to reject the bait. This action caused the angled barb to penetrate the fish's cheek and hook it.

Other Fishing Methods

Herring were also part of the bounty of the sea along the Northwest Coast. They are a small fish, 10 or 12 inches (25 or 30 centimeters) long, and swarm through the surf while spawning in the early spring. They are used for bait, eaten fresh (even raw), and smoked or dried in long strings. The device used in their harvest is called a herring rake though it resembles a giant long-handled comb with extra short teeth. A pole, approximately four yards (3.6 meters) in length, had a line of sharp bone teeth set in the outer one-third. Women paddled their husbands in canoes along the shallow beaches that teemed with spawning herring in season. The men swept the herring rake through the school of fish in a J-stroke making the final upturn quite swiftly. Perhaps a dozen herring at a time would be impaled on the bone teeth. A sharp rap of the handle over the gunnel knocked the fish into the bottom of the canoe, and the rake was then quickly returned to the water before the school was lost. In this manner, a canoe could be filled with fish in a short time. Various styles of seines and dip nets were also effectively used during the herring run.

The eggs of herring were in high esteem as a delicacy and were either eaten raw or dried. The Indians usually served them with seal oil. Leaves of the kelp plant covered with the roe were harvested. In early March, weighted hemlock branches were also placed along beaches and in bays that were known to be good spawning areas. The herring deposited their eggs in a gelatinous coating on these branches. A few days later, the branches, heavily laden with spawn, were collected and taken back to camp to be eaten or dried for future use.

The eulachon run preceded that of the herring by a couple of weeks. Their arrival in river mouths was heralded by the raucous calling of hoards of seagulls. This was the first harbinger of spring for these people who were weary of the long winter months. The eulachon, a silvery 8 or 10 inch (20 to 25 centimeter) fish, represented a reprieve from a rather steady winter diet of dried or smoked salmon. Now fresh fish was available. But it was the oil from these fish that was of the greatest value. Also known as the "candle-fish," a dried eulachon could be lit on one end and burned because its oil content was so high.

Herring rakes were used from canoes during the herring spawning run in early spring.

Eulachon were harvested with herring rakes, seines, and dip nets. Large funnel-shaped bag nets were anchored to the bottom with poles holding the mouth open. The tidal drift filled these bag nets with eulachon. All of the methods that were effective on eulachon were also used on smelt in season.

Canoe loads of eulachon were placed in earth pits and allowed to "ripen" for a couple of weeks. This was the first step in the oil-rendering process. When the fish had decayed sufficiently — the exact length of time depended on the weather — this rancid lot was transferred to a canoe partially buried for stabilization. This canoe served as a large rendering vat. Water was added to the fish and the whole concoction was brought to a boil by adding hot rocks. When the rocks cooled, they were removed. Constant agitation by stirring the mixture helped the fish oil to separate and float to the top. This oil layer was siphoned off and stored in long tubes made from the hollow kelp plant stem. The residue in the bottom of the canoe was dipped out and placed on a grate over a wooden container and pressed to extract the maximum amount of precious oil. Eulachon oil was a condiment for many foods. It was also such an important trade commodity that the inland routes used for trading became known as "grease trails". Eulachon not used for extracting oil were dried or smoked for future use. In the smoke houses and on drying racks, they would be hung in pairs, the head of one fish pulled through the gills of another.

Ling cod was a species of lesser importance to the coastal people; but, nonetheless, considerable originality was exercised in their harvest. Smaller tom cod, their gullets stuffed with gravel, were trolled behind canoes. Ling cod grabbed this bait, and were immediately given some slack line by the fisherman. This permitted the small weighted tom cod to be swallowed and the large cod fish could then be gently pulled into the canoe.

Eulachon that were not rendered for oil were hung in pairs on racks to dry — the head of one pulled through the gills of another.

Throat gorges, though simple in design, were effective in use. They were made of straight pieces of bone or copper, pointed on each end, and usually grooved in the center for a line tie. Their use was not limited to Northwest Coast groups but was widely distributed over North America. Strips of bait were threaded over the gorge. After being swallowed, any resistance on the line would cause the gorge to move crossways in the fish's gullet. Several gorges on short leaders of sinew, doeskin or nettle fiber were used for fishing on the bottom from a weighted-kelp main line.

Throat gorges were indigenous to a number of areas in addition to the Northwest Coast.

Considerable inventiveness was evident in the codfish lure. Shaped similarly to a modern day badminton shuttle-cock, this cleverly devised wooden decoy was pushed vertically underwater with a long pole. The lure was dislodged with a jerk and the pole was quickly withdrawn. The buoyant sham fish then upended itself and started slowly floating towards the surface. The blades were designed to cause the lure to revolve in tantalizing fashion as it rose. Curious codfish were then speared as they followed the lure to the boat.

Flounder, though much smaller in size, resemble halibut in their general shape and bottom-dwelling preference, and usually inhabit shallow, muddy estuaries and bays. Young lads considered it great sport to locate these fish on the bottom with their bare feet while wading, and then spear them.

A codfish swims over to investigate a twirling codfish lure.

Octopus known as devil fish were an important bait source. A special spear was constructed for devil fish. It had a single sharp point with an angled barb on the end of a fairly long shaft. Probing with this spear among rock piles and down in the crevices between rocks would locate devil fish in their favorite haunt. The soft globular mass of the octopus was easily distinguished from the surrounding rocks. The octopus further confirmed its presence by hunching up in response to the spear point prodding its back. At this moment the spear was thrust into the octopus. A steady pull was exerted, not too much so as to tear the barb loose from the flesh, and gradually the devil fish would tire and release its suction grip on the rocks.

The single-barbed octopus spear was used to impale and retrieve octopus from off-shore rock piles.

A Kwakiutl man has speared an octopus or devil fish.

Sturgeon were the largest of all freshwater fish. These modern survivors from pre-civilization times could be twenty feet (6 meters) long and weigh nearly a ton (900 kilograms). Salish tribes along the Columbia and Fraser Rivers were adept at harpooning these leviathans from their deep-water lairs. They were harpooned much like salmon during the summer months when spawning in the shallows. In the winter, however, sturgeon stayed in deep pockets of the river and were quite sluggish. At this time specialized techniques were required. Dual-prong harpoons with detachable heads on shafts of perhaps 40 or 50 feet (12 or 15 meters) in length were used. Two men in a canoe slowly drifted stern first down a section of river. The paddler controlled the canoe while the harpooner in the bow skillfully probed the river bottom for resting sturgeon by raising and lowering his long harpoon as the canoe advanced. A sudden thrust was made as soon as the sturgeon was felt on the bottom and the toggles, attached by their lanyard to the canoe, were disengaged from the shaft.

This long-handled harpoon with dual prongs was used on sturgeon in their deep water lairs.

During the probing, this same lanyard was kept taut to aid in keeping the long shaft vertical in the current. Once subdued, the sturgeon was usually towed to shore for butchering. If the sturgeon needed to be brought into the canoe for transport, an outrigger consisting of a block of wood on a pole was lashed across the gunwales to balance the craft during loading. An alternate method that required some expertise involved tipping over the canoe and scooping the sturgeon up within. The righted canoe was then bailed out and paddled home.

Sea Otter Hunting

Sea otters were a commodity of secondary importance prior to the Russian fur trade, but were nonetheless harvested for their velvety fur even in prehistoric times. Apparently the white man's velvet reminded Northwest Coast tribes of luxurious sea otter fur, as the Sailishan trade name was identical for these two items. These marine mammals lived in kelp beds. The depth of ocean and type of rocky bottom favored by kelp plants was also an ideal habitat for abalone and other mollusks, which served as food for sea otters. Sea Otters could be found as far as kelp beds extended offshore, sometimes up to twenty miles (32 kilometers). They dove to the bottom to retrieve clams and then, floating on their backs with a kelp frond wrapped around a hind leg to keep them from drifting with the current, used their stomachs as a work table to crack open their catch with the aid of a rock. Sea otters were one of the few mammals who employ an element of their environment as a tool.

Sea otter pups, napping peacefully in the afternoon sun among the kelp plants, were snatched by Indians quietly sneaking up on them in a canoe. Northwest Coast canoe paddles characteristically had pointed blades. Hence, the water ran off quickly and quietly when the paddle was withdrawn from the water and helped the natives' furtive approach. The surprised and frightened pups, once grabbed and brought into the canoe, would yelp. The parents immediately responded to these distress cries, abandoning all caution in trying to rescue their pups. While circling the canoe they were easily shot, harpooned or even clubbed with a paddle.

The Kwakiutl and Tlingit harpooned hair seals at night along the shorelines of islands. They could be seen swimming underwater at night because of the phosphorescence of their bodies in the water. Sometimes hair seals could be lured in closer to the canoe by moving the paddle edgewise in the water. The paddle, like the seal, glowed with phosphorescence, attracting the hair seal. The most difficult part of the operation was to keep the harpoon line from tangling in the kelp as the seal swam through it.

Smithsonian Institution — Photo by A.K. Fisher, June 1899

Stretched seal skins dry at a Tlingit hunter's camp on the south shore of Yakutat Bay, Alaska.

Whaling

Most Northwest Coast tribes were content to butcher an occasional beached whale. The Nootkas of Vancouver Island and the Makahs of the Olympic Peninsula were exceptions. They were true seafaring whalers and actively pursued these ocean giants from their canoes. Their crafts were seaworthy and their gear capable. Their knowledge of the California gray whale and its habitat was extensive and their dedication to this dangerous task keen. The harpoon heads usually had razor-sharp shell blades with a split elk antler tine serving as a barb. These were lashed together and covered with pitch to make a smooth surface. Braided bear intestine made a strong harpoon line and was attached, not to the canoe, but rather to inflated sealskin floats.

Smithsonian Institution — Photo by Asabel Curtis 1909

A Makah whaler (Lighthouse Jim) poses with his whaling outfit.

A Makah whaler attaches his harpoon point. Floats fastened to the line are in the foreground.

The whaling canoe carried a crew of eight with the head man being the harpooner. This position was granted to a chief or person of high tribal standing and wealth. Such glamorous and important positions became the birthrights of the sons of chiefs.

Once a whale was spotted, the canoe was maneuvered alongside, and as the mammal reached the surface, the harpoon was thrust into it. Once the whale was struck, each crew member, from harpooner to helmsman, had a specific task to perform, with the utmost synchronization required. Certain crew members started paddling rapidly away from the whale so as to avoid the lashing tail of the wounded animal. Other crew members let out the harpoon line with its three attached sealskin floats, all the while being careful not to get an arm or leg caught in a loop of line, as this meant certain amputation. The sealskin floats slowed the whale's flight, and whenever there was the opportunity, another harpoon with its additional floats was thrust into the whale.

The safety of the crew and the success of the hunt were thought to depend on proper pre-hunt ritual preparation. Even after the whale was struck, an incantation was sung beseeching the victim's cooperation in swimming toward shore rather than out to sea: "Whale, I have given you what you are wishing to get — my good harpoon. And now you have it. Please hold it with your strong hands and do not let go. Whale, turn toward the beach and you will be proud to see the young men come down to see you; and the young men will say to one another: 'What a great whale he is! What a fat whale he is! What a strong whale he is!' And you, whale, will be proud of all that you will hear them say of your greatness. Whale, do not turn outward but hug the shore, and tow me to the beach of my village, for when you come ashore there; the young men will cover your great body with bluebill duck feathers and with the down of the great eagle, the chief of all birds; for this is what you are wishing, and this is what you are trying to find from one end of the world to the other, every day you are traveling and spouting."

More often than not, the initial stick with the harpoon was followed by a long and perilous tug-of-war in which

Smithsonian Institution — circa 1926

A Makah whaling crew prepare to beach a whale at Neah Bay, Washington. Sealskin floats help keep the carcass afloat.

seamanship and raw courage counted far more than flowery incantations. Eventually, the great leviathan tired from the resistance offered by the sealskin floats and the whalers could approach their prize. The first task was to sever the tendons of the tail lobes and flippers to prevent the whale from sounding again. Several canoes were summoned to tow the whale back to camp where it was butchered. The saddle of blubber under the dorsal fin traditionally belonged to the harpooner. During excavations of the Ozette site, one of the finest items recovered was a carved wooden dorsal fin of a whale with the underlying saddle of blubber. The relic, decorated with sea otter teeth, was undoubtedly symbolic of the ultimate whaling trophy of some proud Makah harpooner.

Land Mammal
and Bird Hunting

Nowhere was there a non-agricultural people who depended less on the hunting of land mammals than did those living along the Northwest Coast. Dogs, however, were occasionally trained to drive the small blacktail deer out of the forests and down onto the beach where they were handicapped in the surf, and were easy prey for hunters with spears or bows and arrows. Some early documentary paintings of coastal scenes depicted small white poodle-like dogs that were specially bred for their fur, which was used in weaving. These may have been the same dogs trained to run deer. Other more traditional methods of hunting deer were also used.

Mountain goats were important for their fur, which was woven into chilcat blankets, and for their horns which were ornately carved into ladle handles. Hunting these agile dwellers of craggy peaks and precipitous ledges required using the terrain to the hunter's advantage. Snares were set along narrow ledges where there was not enough room to side-step the loop. By climbing above a herd of goats and slowly ambling down a ridge towards them, the hunters could coax the animals into a blind canyon where they were penned and killed. Mountain goats had a particular tenacity for life and were difficult to kill. Goat hunters designed special rankling tips with multiple barbs for hunting the sinewy animals. The theory was that once penetration was made with the tip, the multiple barbs would work the point further into the animal during its contortions while attempting to escape. Eventually a vital organ would be penetrated and the animal would die. From an anatomical standpoint, the feasibility of a rankling point performing in this manner seems a bit far-fetched.

Wolves, foxes, weasels, and even bears were caught in deadfall traps. Marmots, ground squirrels, and rabbits fell prey to snares made of sinew. The nooses of these snares were held open by trap sticks made of bone, and often sported an animal carved in typical Northwest Coast style on their top.

Mountain goats.

Winter was a time of particularly heavy concentrations of waterfowl along the Northwest Coast. At this time the area became the resort of countless ducks and geese taking refuge from the inhospitable winter conditions to the north and east. They were hunted from blinds with blunt-tipped stunning arrows. Salish tribes hung fine nets woven from nettle fiber from poles along favorite flight paths. This almost invisible net barrier sometimes extended as much as 40 feet (12 meters) into the air and was successful in entangling many species of ducks as well as shorebirds.

Twentieth-century affluence and technology make the natural abundance of the Northwest Coast seem paltry. For primitive man, however, this gale-whipped conjunction of land and sea, was a land of plenty that made possible one of the world's most elaborate primitive cultures.

Lynx Tom Hall

Hunters of the Eastern Forests

The great eastern hardwood forest was a marvelous wilderness before it was transformed by axe and plow, and became a sacrifice to the goddess of technical civilization and progress. Beech, basswood, maple, American chestnut, elm, wild cherry and ash covered the great area north of the Mason-Dixon Line from the Mississippi River to the Atlantic Coast. In this great forest, deer, black bear, eastern cougar and wild turkey thrived. This was the land of the Eastern Woodland Indian Culture with tribes, or nations, such as the Miami, Illinois, Huron, Potawatomi and Delaware. The culture area ascribed to the Eastern Woodland Indians goes beyond the deciduous hardwood forests of the eastern United States, crosses the transition forests of scrub oak and pine, and includes the coniferous forests of southcentral and southeastern Canada. Here, in a land of pine and birch, is the home of the Chippewa, Fox, Sauk, Menominee, Winnebago and Ottawa — all a part of the Eastern Woodland Culture.

The Woodland Indians have never sparked interest in the manner of the Sioux, Blackfoot, Crow and other Western Plains tribes. Nor have native art aficionados been interested in Eastern Woodland items as much as they have in the pottery of the Pueblos or in Navajo rugs. Perhaps most public familiarity with Woodland Indians is through the *Leatherstocking Tales* of James Fenimore Cooper or Longfellow's *Hiawatha*.

Being the first to greet settlers entering the new world, this culture was also the first to be introduced to smallpox, tuberculosis, alcoholism, and other scourges of the whiteman. The acculturation of Woodland Indians into white society was so rapid and complete that a shortage of good descriptive accounts of life before the whiteman has resulted.

Indians of the Eastern Woodlands were semi-nomadic; although they maintained permanent villages, seasonal cycles still necessitated frequent movement. They successfully raised corn, beans and squash, and gathered nuts, berries, wild rice, and maple sugar. Such horticultural-gathering practices were the primary means of subsistence. Hunting and fishing were supplementary to the natives' food quest, although these, too, were of great importance. The Indians of the Eastern forests were about the most accomplished outdoorsmen the world has ever known.

Smithsonian Institution

The Assiniboine, like most Eastern Woodland tribes, were semi-nomadic. Here a hunter uses pack dogs to enhance his mobility.

The hunters of the Eastern Woodlands were expert at deciphering all that had transpired on the forest floor.

The silence and stealth with which they stalked their prey has become part of the American Legend. They could make themselves almost invisible among their surroundings and move in ghost-like fashion along a game trail. Their spear or bow was ever-ready for immediate action, and they could freeze into immobility, remaining motionless for long periods of time if necessary. Patience was perhaps the deadliest of their weapons. They hunted in almost total silence. Even when they sat about the campfire and talked of their hunting exploits, they did so in a low tone of voice as if the animals were listening. A lifetime of attention to details in the wilds enabled them to determine if a set of tracks were left by a male or female, how large the animal was, how fast it was traveling, and how long ago it had passed. Clues might consist of overturned pebbles, minor depressions in leaf cover or grass, snapped twigs or other miniscule disturbances on the forest floor. An occasional speck of blood or soft dropping was a bonus find. Though this might all seem like magic to the modern Nimrod, their system was based on total logic.

Big Game Hunting

The primary weapons of the Eastern Woodland Indians were bows and arrows and spears. Of the two, certainly spears have the greatest antiquity. The hand-thrown spear became an entirely different weapon with the advent of the spear thrower or *atlatl*, as they were called in Central America. The story of the origin of this device has been lost through the ages, but they were definitely used throughout the Americas. Called throwing boards in the Arctic, and differing in design from those used farther south, they existed in the north country until well after white contact. Elsewhere, they were gradually replaced by the more sophisticated and effective bow and arrow. Carved antler tips that served as the hooked ends on atlatls are not rare archaeological finds in the eastern United States, attesting to their use by Woodland Indians. Typically having handles made of wood, and a tip of bone or antler, atlatls were approximately 18 inches (46 centimeters) in length. The antler or bone end-piece had a small projection designed to fit into a recession in the butt of the spear. The atlatl was retained in the hand as the spear was thrown, but greatly increased its velocity by lengthening the radius of the casting arc of the thrower's arm. With the addition of the atlatl, the hand-thrown spear became an effective, lethal weapon.

Like atlatls, bows were present throughout the North and South American continents when white men first arrived. Their lengths, styles, construction and capabilities varied greatly from area to area. Such differences, plus a wide geographical dispersion of bows and arrows, make the theory of several scattered and independent inventions of the weapon quite plausible. Bows used by Woodland Indians were, for the most part, longer than those used in other parts of the country. Hickory and white ash were the preferred bow woods although hop hornbean (ironwood) and red cedar were also used. Bow strings were made from twisted bear intestine or from woodchuck hide. Arrowheads were usually made of flint, but bone was also used.

In spite of a somewhat sophisticated weaponry, the killing power and range of the Eastern Indian's arsenal was still quite limited. Long and diligent stalks were necessary to get within effective range of an intended quarry. More often than not, an additional long episode of tracking was required after the animal was struck in order to find the wounded game, as there were few instant kills. Interestingly, even after acquisition of white man's firearms, most Indians were poor long-range shots despite legends to the contrary. It was still necessary for them to rely on their great skill of silent stalking and tracking, and the ability to conceal themselves in order to procure game.

Realizing that they could rarely track an animal right to where it slept, they paid almost as much attention to the trail ahead as they did to the ground below their feet. A thorough knowledge of the terrain and habits of the animals being pursued eliminated unproductive meanderings along the trail. Rather than doggedly following tracks, the hunter would go directly to points the animal was likely to pass, and pick up the trail again. This technique allowed considerable time and distance to be gained on an animal.

The Indians paid meticulous attention to wind currents as all good hunters must. They were aware of the phenomenon that on windless days cold air in the valleys was warmed by the morning sun and would rise carrying scents with it. Accordingly, in the mornings, they would hunt from higher elevations down towards the valley floors. In the evening, as the air became cooler, the process was reversed. Observations of the behavior of ground fog undoubtedly was responsible for this information.

The practice of rapidly tracking and pursuing an

animal until it reached the point of total exhaustion was common among Eastern Woodland Cultures. Relays of young, fleet-footed runners were formed to relentlessly chase a frightened animal. Knowing in advance the probable attempted escape route of the animal, fresh runners were posted along the way to carry on the chase. The exhausted animal, its fright draining its strength, eventually collapsed and was an easy kill. Being the opportunists they were, Indian hunters listened for the cries of a marauding wolf pack signaling a deer chase was underway. With the task of wearing the deer down already initiated by the wolves, Indian runners would take up the chase and claim the spoils in the end. In some eastern tribes, young, unmarried men were specifically trained to become runners. They were members of a sort of fraternity with strict rules of conduct, rigorous physical training, and much spiritual preparation.

Deer drives were effective in pushing a deer into a situation of distinct advantage for the hunter, such as a promontory of land extending into a lake or river. Here the deer was forced to plunge into the water, and the pursuit was continued by Indians in swift and agile birchbark canoes. Once overtaken in the water, the animal was readily dispatched with the sharp edge of a canoe paddle swung against the base of the animal's skull. Lances and, as some evidence suggests, even harpoons were also used. Chance encounters with deer or moose voluntarily crossing deep water occurred, and these animals, too, were intercepted and slaughtered.

Human scent was just as effective in driving deer as was actual sight of a line of advancing drivers. For this reason, the day for the drive was carefully selected on the basis of wind direction and weather conditions. Intentionally set fires were utilized at strategic points to help herd the frightened animal towards its rendezvous with death. It is a quirk of animal behavior that deer are particularly terrified by the smell of scorched flesh. Indian drivers often enhanced the effectiveness of their own dreaded human scent by carrying pieces of burned meat on sticks.

Smithsonian Institution — Photo by Roland Reed circa 1900

Chippewa men pursue a deer that has been driven into the water.

In deer drives, scent and visibility were purposely made obvious to the quarry; in ambush tactics every attempt was made to conceal both the sight and smell of the hunter. Indian hunters were astute observers of the natural world, and understood animal behavior well. They knew places frequented by deer and moose such as favorite watering areas, mineral licks, bedding areas, and scrapes. They also understood how to utilize these areas to their benefit by properly placing blinds where effective close-range attacks could be carried out.

In another method that was really a combination of stalking and ambushing, the blind was actually carried to the deer themselves. This involved wearing a tanned deerskin, with antlers attached, and moving into the center

By draping themselves with a deer cape, Indian hunters were able to make a closer approach to their quarry.

of a feeding herd of deer. Ethnologists have long recognized that animals of a given species recognize each other by prominent parts of the body rather than by the animal as a whole. Characteristic postures and gaits also play an important role in this animal identification. Tribes as diverse as the Iroquois of the East and the Maidu of central California took advantage of this to get close to deer. Walking in a crouched-over position with their bow and bundle of arrows dangling down in such a manner as to resemble forelegs, the hunter advanced when the deer's head was down browsing. Approaches from the side took advantage of the deer's limited peripheral vision, and prevented too close scrutiny. A direct rear approach would frighten the timid deer and was avoided. The hunter's chest was painted white to correspond with a deer's underside.

Milwaukee Public Museum

An Ojibwa lady scrapes a stretched deer hide with a section of a gun barrel flattened on one end.

This technique was best employed during the rut. A little grating of bow and arrow shafts together simulated the sound of bucks intermeshing their antlers, and might bring a buck deer a few steps closer if judiciously used at just the right moment.

A variation of this technique was used by the Chickasaw and Choctaw of the middle gulf region, and probably eastern tribes as well. They would use a deer head on their fist, much as one would work a hand puppet, to imitate the feeding movements of deer, and hence coax the animals closer. Deer heads used in this way consisted of a cured skin and the frontal bone of the deer's skull with the antlers attached. The antlers were meticulously hollowed out to make them lighter. The cape was stretched over split cane hoops to give it form, and a hand-hold extended from the inner surface of the frontal bone.

The reflexes of some game animals, particularly white-tailed deer, are so quick that they will literally "jump the string" or get out of the way in the minute time interval elapsing between the twang of the bowstring and the instant that the arrow arrives at its mark. This was especially true in the close-range stalking that the Indians of the Eastern forests had to do. Tufts of downy feathers tied to the bowstring acted as silencers. Characteristically, owl feathers were used because this predatory bird was known to be a silent hunter on the wing, and it was hoped that the owl's hushed manner would become a property of the bow.

Certain types of ambush hunting had their effectiveness enhanced by the use of animal calls. A wooden device with a hole cut in the center that was partially covered by a thin piece of fish skin would, when blown on, emit a sound like the tremulous bleating of a fawn. This sound attracted does as well as many predators. Sounds that represented no specific animal or bird, such as scratching, soft whistling or quiet tapping, often piqued the curiosity of game, and brought them to within range of the Indian hunter.

Jack-lighting deer at night from a canoe with a fire on a flat stone placed in the bow was commonly practiced throughout the Great Lakes area.

Several Great Lakes area tribes hunted deer by "jack-lighting" after dark. A fire was built on a flat stone placed in the bow of a canoe. Another flat stone placed upright acted as a reflecting shield behind the fire. The canoe was silently paddled about the shore of a lake while the hunter crouched behind the reflecting stone so as not to be temporarily blinded by the light of the fire. Once located, deer were intrigued by the strange light, and stood motionless staring into it. This resulted in a temporary blindness, and allowed close approach of the canoe for an easy shot. Even those deer that were not transfixed by the light and fled would, as often as not, become confused by their own leaping shadows and run towards the hunter. Hand-carried torches permitted essentially the same type of hunting on land. Torches were fashioned out of pitch-laden pine knots on the end of a limb which served as a handle, or of a green stave split at one end to hold a bundle of folded birch-bark strips.

"Jerking a deer" Notice unskinned doe heads on each end of the pole frame and over the embers.

Snares attached to bent saplings, or "springpoles," were set on deer trails and sprung when a delicate trigger mechanism was activated. A simpler and more effective deer trap, however, consisted of a brush barrier across the game trail. Deer effortlessly leaped across this obstruction, but waiting for them on the opposite side was a sharpened stake set in the ground on which they landed and became impaled.

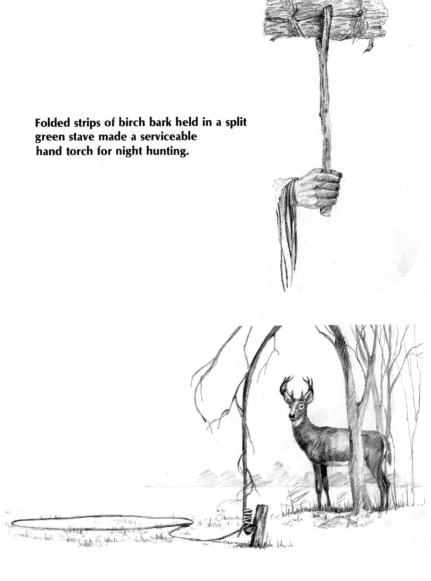

Folded strips of birch bark held in a split green stave made a serviceable hand torch for night hunting.

Springpole snares were set in game trails.

It is uncertain just how often moose were killed by Woodland Culture Indians prior to the advent of modern weapons, but those periods in which the animals were vulnerable were taken advantage of. One such period was the rut, when the moose's libido is at high pitch. Moose, particularly love-sick bulls, were called into effective range during the rut with a series of amorous "grunts" amplified by a birch bark megaphone. Calling was frequently done either concealed on the shore of a lake or from a canoe. The final "come-on" was elicited by filling the moose call or a canoe bailer with water and allowing it to slowly and noisily trickle back into the lake. This sounded to the bull moose like water dripping off the muzzle of a cow as she lifted her head from eating under-water plants in the lake, or better yet, like the cow moose urinating in the lake and thus indicating her willingness. Such sensual "moose talk" usually sufficed to lure the bull from his cover in a final rage of passion. When calling from a canoe on the lake, the shortsighted moose frequently mistook the craft with its hunter as the object of his intentions, and some very close encounters resulted.

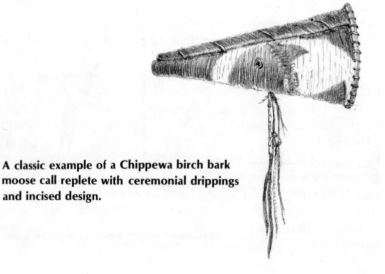

A classic example of a Chippewa birch bark moose call replete with ceremonial drippings and incised design.

State Historical Society of Wisconsin — Photo by Roland Reed.

An Ojibwa hunter uses a birch bark megaphone to call moose from his canoe.

The shoulder blade of a moose was often used in calling to supplement the birch bark-megaphone type of call. The scapula of a female moose was favored for superstitious reasons, or perhaps because that of the bull was just too heavy to carry around. After its dorsal ridge had been trimmed off, the scapula was hung up to dry. The altered shoulder blade was rubbed against a tree, mimicking the sound bulls often make during their sham fights with a tree or bush during the rut. A fresh bone could be used if necessary, but these lacked the desired qualities or resonance. When hunters found a clump of bushes which had been raked or scraped of their bark, or when fresh spoor was sighted, they would use their scapula. Long periods of silent listening always followed each use. Moose calls were traditionally hidden from women and children for

fear of ritual contamination. Some of the birch bark calls were elaborately decorated with ceremonial drippings and incised designs in the cambium layer of the bark.

The Penobscot preferred to hunt moose when there was a heavy snow cover. At such times, their webbed footgear gave them a distinct advantage in mobility. The strategy was to wound a moose with a spear or arrow when it was first sighted, usually in its wintering yard, where there

272

A bull moose is lured to within bow range with amorous grunts made with a birch bark moose call.

was not much snow. The wounded animal would flee its sanctuary, and to follow it across deep drifts was a simple matter. The hunter got in another shot whenever possible and, all the while, drove the animal toward areas of deeper snow. Eventually, the moose, with its great weight and sharp hooves, would flounder and become easy prey for its snowshoe-clad tormentors.

It is legend that primitive man from diverse cultures across the continent looked upon the bear with feelings of veneration and awe. Perhaps it was the close resemblance to the human form when standing on its hind feet that evoked this brotherly reverence towards the bear. Nevertheless, they were killed for their meat, hide and the claws which were used to make highly prized necklaces. For some reason, few good descriptive accounts of bear hunting have been preserved. Being a semi-hibernator, black bears were best subdued in their winter lairs. In the hardwood forests, standing hollow trees were favored as dens. When suitable trees were not available, likely denning sites included the area beneath a ledge of rocks, under the roots of a partly fallen tree or in a rocky crevice on a mountainside. Dens were usually on a high elevation with a south-facing slope. Such a location stayed clear longer in the autumn, opened earlier with the melting snows of spring and afforded adequate drainage. Likely denning sites were located and memorized during the Indian hunters' foragings in the woods throughout the year, and were then re-visited in March or April. Fresh claw marks on the trunk of a tree indicated current habitation. The bear was routed from its quarters either with poles thrust into the den or by smoke. Aroused from a deep sleep, the bear was stuporous and sudden exposure to bright sunlight was blinding at first. Under such conditions, the black bear would not make a very formidable adversary and was easily killed.

Baiting may have been used in hunting black bear, and there are sporadic reports of dogs being used by the Creek Indians although this may have been solely in the post-contact era.

Elk once inhabited the East in mountainous sections of Pennsylvania, West Virginia, and Ohio. The last wild elk reported in West Virginia was seen in Pocahontas County in 1845. There was also a species of woods buffalo found in the Eastern forest. Only scant information remains, but it is logical to assume that these animals were hunted by the same general methods of driving, stalking, and ambushing that were successfully employed on other big game animals.

Small Game Hunting

The larger game animals provided most of the staples necessary for existence, but many small mammals were also taken both for food and for the use of their pelts. Otter fur in particular was valued as a covering for bow cases and quivers, for medicine bundles and as hair wrappings. Beaver hunting was mostly an ancillary undertaking prior to the influence of white fur traders. An insatiable demand for beaver fur in Europe in the 1600's and 1700's spurred traders in their quest for riches through the fur trade. A heavier beaver kill by the Indians was encouraged, and more efficient methods were devised. No longer was the shooting of a solitary beaver or otter as it swam across a pond sufficient. Entire colony-decimating tactics were probably used on occasion before white contact, but not on the grand scale that was encouraged by the early fur traders.

Winter was the ideal time to hunt beavers, and this coincided with the time when their fur was at its prime. The first step in these brutally successful hunts was to locate all of the burrows or "washes" along the shore of a beaver pond that led up underneath the bank. This was accomplished by thumping the ice around the banks and thus sounding out the burrow when a change in pitch occurred. All the exits from any beaver house in the pond were also located. Since these were usually in deep water

The winter beaver hunt involved the whole tribe and all phases had to be closely synchronized for success.

and were therefore more difficult to "tap out," they were often marked by stakes before the pond froze over. Any creek flowing into or out of the pond was picketed from side to side with stakes to prevent passage. A hole was then chopped in the ice directly over each burrow and at each lodge exit. A hunter was posted by each hole. When everyone was set to satisfaction, attention was turned to the main lodge itself. This was broken into from the frozen top, and the sticks and mud were jammed into each opening or exit. This was done to prevent the beavers from returning once they had been routed from the lodge. If several lodges were present in a single pond, they were all opened simultaneously in this fashion. The beaver fled via their usual routes to the burrows under the bank which they used for breathing places and as a sanctuary if they were disturbed at their lodge. It was then the duty of each hunter stationed at a hole to either snatch barehanded or to net any beaver that attempted escape beneath the hole. The startled beavers were jerked from the water at the critical moment as they passed beneath the hole, and were hurled onto the ice and rapidly clubbed. If the hunters had been thorough in locating exits and burrows, no avenue of escape remained, and the entire colony was annihilated. The young beavers were generally the first killed while older adults were more adept at avoiding the holes where hunters were stationed. Not infrequently, a wise old beaver might successfully obtain temporary sanctuary in a burrow among the roots of a large tree up under the bank. Dogs were then used to identify the occupied burrows, and the beaver resident was put to flight back through the passageways under holes in the ice.

To preserve the proper water level in their ponds, beavers kept a zealous watch over their dams and made periodic checks on the structure to make sure all was in order. The effect of any sudden fall in water level immediately brought beavers scurrying to the dam to make necessary repairs. Indians took advantage of this and used it to the beaver's destruction. After purposefully destroying a part of the dam and allowing water to escape, the Indians would remain downwind and out of sight and shoot the little builders as they came to make their repairs.

Muskrat (*Musquash*) meat was relished even more than beaver meat, and their pelts were also useful. Eastern Woodland Indians used a muskrat call made with a device consisting of two pieces of wood, each about three inches (8 centimeters) long, mortised at each end. An opening was left in the center between them, and a shred of birch bark was fastened through the middle. Blowing through this device produced a resonant buzzing which resembled the call of a muskrat. By paddling their canoe along the shore of a lake, or still sections of a river where muskrats were plentiful, and working their call, Indians lured muskrats out from the bank to the canoe. The rats were then killed by a blow on the head with a canoe paddle. This call apparently worked so well that occasionally a muskrat was so deceived that it would try to clamber up into the canoe, evidently mistaking it for a log.

This method of hunting required two hunters in the canoe for best results, one to work the call and one to swing the paddle. It was necessary to stay downwind and to remain as motionless as possible. All the communications that were needed between hunters were accomplished by a mere shake of the canoe or a slight nod of the head.

The muskrat call, though simply devised with two pieces of wood containing a piece of birch bark or fish skin, was effective in luring muskrats to a close range.

Muskrat house construction was not unlike that of beavers in basic design except it was on a smaller scale and utilized grass and mud instead of the heavier limbs and small trees incorporated into the beaver lodges. The interior of the little mud-cave house was a hollow saucer-shaped area elevated just above the water level. The entrance was underwater. In the winter, a muskrat family would huddle close together in this area for warmth, often one on top of another. As soon as the ice was solid enough to support the weight of a hunter, a form of winter muskrat hunting began. After quietly approaching the muskrat house with spear poised, a mighty thrust was made blindly through the center of the lodge. If a rat was pierced, its wriggling was felt through the spear handle. The hunter maintained pressure against the spear shaft to keep his quarry pinned while the mud and grass of the lodge was torn away. The muskrat was then grabbed by the tail, removed from the spear and knocked against the ice. Not infrequently, the spear passed through two or even three of the muskrats in one stroke.

The crossing of a fresh lynx track in the wilds would always precipitate a chase. As soon as the lynx realized that it was being followed, it would climb a tree. If within bow range the cat was simply shot. If the animal was higher up, the tree was felled. As soon as the tree began to totter, the Indian ran towards the line of fall to be on hand to club the lynx as soon as it crashed to the ground. Most lynx however were caught in snares. The noose was set in a likely place, and the standing portion was attached to a light toss pole. Frequently, a rabbit skin with the head attached was stuffed with moss or snow and set in back of the snare so a lynx would spot this decoy and make a lunge through the noose for it. Once caught, the lynx became its own executioner by standing on the drag and pulling its head back. This attempt at gaining freedom only served to tighten further the noose about the lynx's neck, and hastened its strangulation. Occasionally, a lynx took the drag in its mouth after being caught, and climbed a tree. This invariably would cause its death because once in the tree, the lynx would drop the stick. When it started to descend, the stick would catch in a fork and the lynx would be hung.

Most of the smaller animals inhabiting the Eastern and Northern forests were hunted by stalking and ambushing techniques. Squirrels were hunted with blunt arrows or stunners so less meat was spoiled. Grating two smooth round pebbles together mimicked the sound of a squirrel cutting a hickory nut, and was often successful in persuading a skittish bushytail to raise his head above a limb to peruse the situation. When a cat and mouse game was played between squirrel and hunter about the trunk of a tree, the old "hat trick" of tossing an object over to the squirrel's side of the tree usually worked in bringing the squirrel over to the hunter's side. The arrows used on small game such as squirrels, and also on birds, had the feathers, or fletching, applied in a spiral rather than the usual three straight vanes. This bushy fletching acted like a brake on the arrow, and shortened its maximum range so that it dropped quickly to the ground after a miss and would not be lost.

That simplest of traps, the pitfall, was probably man's earliest device for capturing animals by remote control. In their most primitive form, pitfalls were just a hole in the ground into which an unwary animal might fall and become trapped. As their construction became more sophisticated, camouflage tops, through which the animal would fall, covered the pits, and impaling stakes were sometimes planted in the bottom. Bait was used, but more often the pits were dug where the Indian trapper knew animals were traveling. Beaver and otter, for example, often crossed over land directly from one bend of a stream to another rather than swimming all the way. These trails made ideal locations for pitfalls.

Animals ranging in size from the tiny weasel to the black bear were caught in deadfall traps. The support and triggering mechanism of the deadfall required three pieces of wood suitably shaped and notched. The horizontal member of the "figure 4" device had the bait either fastened around it or hung from its end. The size and weight of the trap depended on the specific animal for which it was set. The placement of the bait in relation to the falling weight was crucial so that a vital part of the animal, usually the head, was pinned. Shelters of bark or limbs were frequently constructed over deadfalls to capitalize on the urge many mammals possess to investigate any cubbyhole or cavern.

A typical Ojibwa deadfall trap.

An effectively deceptive trap for a fisher or mink was made in the cavity of a log, such as an old woodpecker hole. Two sharp wooden spikes were fixed to the rim of the hole so they angled up and into the hole. The trap was baited

Deadfalls, triggered via a "figure 4" mechanism varied in size according to the animal they were set for.

with a piece of fish. When a mink or fisher tried to steal the bait, they were able to squeeze their head past the inwardly slanting spikes, but were caught when they attempted to back out.

Opossums and porcupines, being relatively slow moving and sluggish were run down and clubbed. These easily caught animals served as good emergency rations during lean times. Young hunters were trained in killing woodchucks in preparation for larger animals and more important hunts later in life. The object was to get between the woodchuck and its burrow so that an interception could be made when the animal ran for the safety of its hole. This tactic also worked on badgers. A favorite method of dispatching this animal was for the hunter to run alongside or just behind the animal, and to jump high and land hard with both feet on the badger's back. This would break the badger's backbone if the hunter was quick and lucky.

Turkeys were lured into bow range with calls, and shot by concealed hunters. Passenger pigeons, now extinct, once roosted in vast flocks in the Eastern forests. These somewhat dull-witted birds were mesmerized by torch light after dark, and enormous numbers of the birds were harvested by knocking them to the ground with long poles.

The Iroquois and Menomini were skilled at luring grouse into a snare by baiting it with grain. A shallow depression in the ground was baited with maize, and this was covered with a piece of elm bark that had a keyhole-shaped opening cut in it. A noose was placed at the apex of the hole. The grain at the wide base of the hole was easily obtained, but to reach those kernels at the top of the hole, the grouse had to stick its neck through the noose. The snare, tangled in the neck feathers, pulled taut when the bird withdrew.

Fishing

The rivers and streams of the eastern United States provided an abundance of fish for the Woodland Indians. They used traps, nets, and spears, but the greatest quantities were probably harvested by poisoning. The root of a plant called devil's shoestring (*Viburnum alnifolium*) was the most common source of poison, although turnip root and poke berry were also used. Devil's shoestring was a common plant growing on the sandy ridges bordering many eastern streams. Several large posts were driven into the stream bed, their tops extending just above the water's surface. The roots that had been gathered were then pulverized with a wooden maul on the tops of the posts. As the mashed roots fell into the water, they exuded their toxins, and the affected fish weakly finned on the surface, gasping for air. Women and children braved the irritating effect the substance had on their skin and waded downstream to gather the fish. Of course, poisoning techniques worked best during periods when rainfall had been light, and the streams were low and sluggish. This was usually in the hot summer months, and at this time the poison was further enhanced by the lowered oxygen content of the warm water.

A Menominee Indian harpooning sturgeon on the Fox River in Eastern Wisconsin.

Certainly plant poisons accounted for the wholesale capture of most fish, but the lone sojourner in the Eastern Forest needed only his bare hands to produce a meal of fresh fish. By feeling gently under submerged ledges and logs, huge catfish could be located. If the angler's touch was delicate, the fish wouldn't flush, and then could be hypnotized with a soft, gentle stroking of its belly. Slowly, the Indian would work his hand into position and grab the fish by its gills. Many years later, old country poachers practiced this art in the same streams, calling it "noodling" or "tickling."

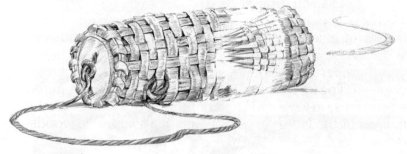

Basket traps such as these were set in rivers for migrating eels. The cutaway shows the conical entrance.

Eels are catadromous, meaning they live in fresh water, but spawn in the ocean. Most Atlantic seaboard rivers had an autumn eel run downstream toward the North Atlantic's Sargasso Sea. Weirs were constructed across rivers to herd the migrating eels onto lattice-work trays just under the water's surface. As they struggled across this shallow barrier, waiting Indians plucked them up and tossed them into a holding pit dug into the sandy bank. The Penobscot and Malecite, in particular, used basket traps with a conical-shaped mouth to catch eels in deeper water. These were baited with fish heads and weighted with rocks to sink them. Wooden floats attached by a line marked their location.

Wading the sluggish sections of streams with muddy bottoms, Woodland Indians located snapping turtles by feeling their backs with their bare feet. They deduced where the head was by the configuration of spines on the turtle's shell. This was important because while the turtle would not open his mouth underwater, his snake-like head was sure to come out snapping in every direction as soon as the animal was brought to the surface. They removed the entrails of the turtles through a cut below the vent, and then placed them on their sides around the fire where they were roasted in their shells.

No Indian cultural group had a more diverse terrain or a greater variety of animal life from which to extract their means of existence than did the Indians of the Eastern Woodlands. For this reason, few cultural groups had a greater repertoire of skills, weapons, or techniques at their disposal. The forest interspersed with open glades fostered an expertise in woodcraft and outdoor lore which made the Indians of the North and East America's supreme woodsmen.

Eastern Woodland Indian fish trap.

Bibliography

Adney, Edwin T., and Chapelle, Howard I. *Bark Canoes and Skin Boats of North America, The.* Washington, D.C.: Smithsonian Institution, 1964.

American West eds. *Great Northwest, The.* Palo Alto, Cal.: American West Publishing Co., 1973.

Bateman, James A. *Animal Traps and Trapping.* Harrisburg, Pa.: Stackpole Books, 1971.

Billard, Jules B., ed. *World of the American Indian, The.* Washington, D.C.: National Geographic Society, 1974.

Billman, Esther, *Eskimo Bird Hunting.* Sitka, Alaska: Sheldon Jackson Museum, 1972.

———. *Eskimo Fishing.* Sitka, Alaska: Sheldon Jackson Museum, 1972.

———. *Eskimo Seal Hunting.* Sitka, Alaska: Sheldon Jackson Museum, 1972.

———. *Eskimo Whale Hunting.* Sitka, Alaska: Sheldon Jackson Museum, 1975.

———. *Tlingit Fishing.* Sitka, Alaska: Sheldon Jackson Museum, 1975.

———. *Tlingit Hunting and Food Preparation.* Sitka, Alaska: Sheldon Jackson Museum, 1975.

Birket-Smith, Kaj. *Eskimos.* New York: Crown Publishers, Inc., 1971.

———. *Eskimos, The.* London: Methuen and Co., Ltd., 1959.

Boas, Franz. *Central Eskimo, The.* 6th Annual Report of The Bureau of American Ethnology, 1884-1885.

———. *Ethnology of the Kwakiutl.* 35th Annual Report of The Bureau of American Ethnology, 1913-1914.

Boudreau, Norman J., ed. *Athapaskans: Strangers of the North, The.* Ottawa, Canada: Catalog for exhibit of National Museum of Man and Royal Scottish Museum, National Museums of Canada, 1974.

Bruemmer, Fred. *Arctic, The.* Montreal, Quebec: Infocor Ltd., 1974.

———. *Seasons of the Eskimo—A Vanishing Way of Life.* Toronto, Ontario: McClelland & Stewart Ltd., 1971.

Catlin, George. *Letters and Notes on the Manners, Customs and Conditions of the North American Indians.* 1832-1839. New York: Dover Publications Inc., 1973.

Chapple, Eliot D., and Coon, Carleton S. *Principles of Anthropology.* New York: Henry Holt & Co. Inc., 1942.

Coon, Carleton S. *Hunting Peoples, The.* Boston: Little, Brown & Co., 1971.

Denig, Edwin T. *Indian Tribes of the Upper Missouri.* 46th Annual Report of The Bureau of American Ethnology. 1928-1929.

Dorsey, J. Owen. *Omaha Sociology.* 3rd Annual Report of The Bureau of American Ethnology. 1881-1882.

Driver, Harold E., and Massey, William C. *Comparative Studies of North American Indians.* Philadelphia, Pa.: The American Philosophical Soc., 1957.

Drucker, Philip. *Cultures of the North Pacific Coast.* San Francisco: Chandler Pub. Co., 1965.

Ellis, Richard. *Book of Whales The.* New York: Alfred A. Knopf, 1980.

Farb, Peter. *Man's Rise to Civilization as Shown by the Indians of North America From Primeval Times to the Coming of the Industrial State.* New York: E.P. Dutton Co. Inc., 1968.

Folsom, Franklin. *America's Ancient Treasures.* New York: Rand McNally & Co., 1961.

Freuchen, Peter. *Book of Eskimos*. Greenwich, Conn.: Fawcett Publications Inc., 1961.

Glist, Valerius. *Neanderthal the Hunter*. Natural History Vol. 90, No. 1, American Museum of Natural History, 1981.

Goddard, P.F. *Indians of the Southwest*. New York: American Museum of Natural History, 1921.

Grinnell, George B. *Cheyenne Indians—Their History and Way of Life, The*. New York: Cooper Square Publishers Inc., 1962.

Haines, Francis, *Buffalo, The*. New York: Thomas Y. Crowell Co., 1970.

Hibben, Frank C. *Lost Americans, The*. New York: Thomas Y. Crowell Co., 1946.

Hill, W.W. *Agricultural and Hunting Methods of the Navaho Indians, The*. Yale University Pub. in Anthropology, Vol. 18, New Haven, Conn.: Yale Univ. Press, 1938.

Hoover, Robert L. *Chumash Fishing Equipment*. San Diego, Calif.: San Diego Museum of Man, 1973.

Hunter, Martin. *Canadian Wilds*. Columbus, Ohio: A.R. Harding, 1935.

Iacopi, Robert L. *Look to the Mountain Top*. San Jose, Calif.: H.M. Gousha Co., 1972.

Jenness, Diamond. *Indians of Canada, The*. Anthropological Series, National Museum of Canada, Ottawa, Canada: 1955.

———. *People of the Twilight*. Chicago, London: Univ. of Chicago Press, 1961.

Josephy, Alvin, M. Jr. *Indian Heritage of America, The*. New York: Alfred A. Knopf, 1968.

Kehoe, Alice B. *Hunters of the Buried Years*. Toronto, Canada: School Aids & Text Book Pub. Co., Ltd.

Knoblock, Byron W. *Banner-stones of the North American Indian*. La Grange, Ill.: Privately published, 1939.

Krause, Aurel. *Tlingit Indians, The*. Seattle, Washington: Univ. of Washington Press, 1885.

LaFarge, Oliver. *A Pictorial History of the American Indian*. New York: Crown Publishers, 1956.

Lee, Richard B., and DeVore, Irven. *Man the Hunter*. Chicago: Aldine Pub. Co., 1968.

Lowie, Robert. *Indians of the Plains*. New York: for The American Museum of Natural History, McGraw-Hill, 1954.

Macfarlan, Allan A. *Modern Hunting with Indian Secrets*. Harrisburg, Pa.: Stackpole Books, 1971.

Mason, Otis T. *Aboriginal American Harpoons: A Study in Ethnic Distribution and Invention*. Annual Report of the U.S. National Museum, Washington, D.C.: 1900.

———. *North American Bows, Arrows and Quivers*. Original Smithsonian Report 1893, Yonkers, N.Y.: Carl J. Pugliese, 1972.

———. *Throwing Sticks in the National Museum*. Smithsonian Annual Report, Vol. 2, 1884.

———. *Traps of the American Indians*. Smithsonian Annual Report, 1901.

Maxwell, James A., ed, and Freed, Stanley A., chief consultant, *America's Fascinating Indian Heritage*. Pleasantville, N.Y.: Reader's Digest Assoc., Inc., 1978.

McClane, A.J. *McClane's New Standard Fishing Encyclopedia*. New York: Holt, Rinehart and Winston, 1974.

McHugh, Tom. *Time of the Buffalo, The*. New York: Alfred A. Knopf Inc., 1972.

Miles, Charles. *Indian & Eskimo Artifacts of North America*. Library of Congress #62-19386, New York: Bonanza Books.

Mowat, Farley. *Desperate People, The*. Boston: Little, Brown & Co., 1959.

———. *People of the Deer*. Boston: Little, Brown & Co., 1952.

289

Murdock, John. *Point Barrow Expedition, The.* 9th Annual Report of the Bureau of American Ethnology, 1887-1888.

Nansen, Fridtjof. *Farthest North.* Vols. I & II, New York: Harper & Brothers, 1897.

———. *Hunting and Adventure in the Arctic.* Duffield & Co., 1925

Nelson, Edward W. *Eskimo About Bering Strait, The.* 18th Annual Report of The Bureau of American Ethnology. 1896-1897.

Nelson, Richard K. *Hunters of the Northern Ice.* Chicago & London: Univ. of Chicago Press, 1969.

———. *Hunters of the Northern Forest.* Chicago & London: Univ. of Chicago Press, 1973.

Norton, Boyd. *Alaska—Wilderness Frontier.* New York: Visual Books, Inc., 1977.

Outdoor Life eds. *Story of American Hunting and Firearms, The.* New York: McGraw-Hill Book Co. Inc., 1959.

Radin, Paul. *Winnebago Tribe, The.* 37th Annual Report of The Bureau of American Ethnology. 1915-1916.

Rasmussen, Knud. *Intellectual Culture of the Copper Eskimos.* Nordisk Forlog, Copenhagen: Gyldendalske Boghandel, 1932.

———. *Intellectual Culture of the Iglulik Eskimos.* Nordisk Forlog, Copenhagen: Gyldendalske Boghandel, 1929.

———. *Netsilik Eskimos, The.* Nordisk Forlog, Copenhagen: Gyldendalske Boghandel, 1932.

Ritzenthaler, Robert E., and Ritzenthaler, Pat. *Woodland Indians of the Western Great Lakes, The.* Garden City, N.Y.: The Natural History Press, 1970.

Ruesch, Hans. *Top of the World.* New York: Harper & Row, 1950.

Russell, Carl P. *Firearms, Traps and Tools of the Mountain Men.* New York: Alfred A. Knopf, Inc., 1967.

Schledermann, Peter. *Eskimo and Viking Finds in the High Arctic.* Vol. 159, No. 5, National Graphic, May 1981.

Speck, Frank G. *Penobscot Man.* Philadephia: University of Pennsylvania Press, 1940.

Stefansson, Vilhjalmur. *My Life With the Eskimos.* New York: Collier Books, 1966.

Stewart, Hilary. *Indian Fishing—Early Methods of the Northwest Coast.* North Vancouver, Canada: J.J. Douglas, Ltd., 1977.

Swanton, John R. *Indians of the Southeastern United States, The.* Smithsonian Institution Bureau of American Ethnology, bulletin #137, Washington, D.C.: U.S. Government Printing Office, 1946.

Teit, James, and Boas, Franz, ed. *Salishan Tribes of the Western Plateaus, The.* 45th Annual Report of The Bureau of American Ethnology. 1927-1928.

Turner, Lucien M., and Murdock, John, ed. *Ethnology of the Ungava District Hudson Bay Territory.* 11th Annual Report of The Bureau of American Ethnology. 1889-1890.

Underhill, Ruth. *Indians of the Pacific Northwest.* Washington, D.C.: The Branch of Education, Bureau of Indian Affairs, 1944.

———. *Red Man's America.* Chicago: Chicago Press, 1953.

Waterman, Charles F. *Hunting in America.* New York: Holt, Rinehart & Winston, 1973.

Wheat, Margaret M. *Survival Arts of the Primitive Paiutes.* Reno, Nev.: University of Nevada Press, 1967.

Index

The Native Hunter Series

by R. Stephen Irwin M.D.

Illustrations by J.B. Clemens

The primary chapters of THE PROVIDERS have been released as five separate books comprising the NATIVE HUNTER SERIES. The series provides a unique glimpse into hunting and fishing technologies of the North American Indians and Eskimos.

Dr. Irwin has brought together years of research in a very informative and readable text, highlighted by dozens of illustrations especially created by renowned artist J.B. Clemens for this series. Many photographs give further insight into the way the first Native Americans lived and hunted.

Hunters of the Buffalo

Hunters of the Eastern Forest

Hunters of the Northern Forest

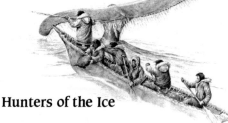

Hunters of the Sea

Hunters of the Ice

OTHER INDIAN TITLES

Ah Mo
Tren J. Griffin
ISBN 0-88839-244-3

American Indian Pottery
Sharon Wirt
ISBN 0-88839-134-X

Argillite: Art of the Haida
Drew & Wilson
ISBN 0-88839-037-8

Art of the Totem
Marius Barbeau
ISBN 0-88839-168-4

Coast Salish
Reg Ashwell
ISBN 0-88839-009-2

Eskimo Life Yesterday
Hancock House
ISBN 0-919654-73-8

Haida: Their Art & Culture
Leslie Drew
ISBN 0-88839-132-3

Hunter Series
By R. Stephen Irwin, MD
Hunters of the Buffalo
ISBN 0-88839-176-5

Hunters of the E. Forest
ISBN 0-88839-178-1

Hunters of the Ice
ISBN 0-88839-179-X

Hunters of the N. Forest
ISBN 0-88839-175-7

Hunters of the Sea
ISBN 0-88839-177-3

Images: Stone: BC
Wilson Duff
ISBN 0-295-95421-3

The Incredible Eskimo
de Coccola & King
ISBN 0-88839-189-7

Indian Art & Culture
Kew & Goddard
ISBN 0-919654-13-4

Indian Artifacts of the NE
Roger W. Moeller
ISBN 0-88839-127-7

Indian Coloring Books
Carol Batdorf

Seawolf
ISBN 0-88839-247-8

Tinka
ISBN 0-88839-249-4

Indian Healing
Wolfgang G. Jilek, MD
ISBN 0-88839-120-X

Indian Herbs
Dr. Raymond Stark
ISBN 0-88839-077-7

Indian Quillworking
Christy Ann Hensler
ISBN 0-88839-214-1

Indian Rock Carvings
Beth Hill
ISBN 0-919654-34-7

Indian Tribes of the NW
Reg Ashwell
ISBN 0-919654-53-3

Indian Weaving, Knitting & Basketry of the NW
Elizabeth Hawkins
ISBN 0-88839-006-8

Iroquois: Their Art & Crafts
Carrie A. Lyford
ISBN 0-88839-135-8

Kwakiutl Legends
Chief Wallas & Whitaker
ISBN 0-88839-094-7

Life with the Eskimo
Hancock House
ISBN 0-919654-72-X

More Ahmo
Tren J. Griffin
ISBN 0-88839-303-2

My Heart Soars
Chief Dan George
ISBN 0-88839-231-1

My Spirit Soars
Chief Dan George
ISBN 0-88839-233-8

NW Native Harvest
Carol Batdorf
ISBN 0-88839-245-1

Power Quest
Carol Batdorf
ISBN 0-88839-240-0

River of Tears
Maud Emery
ISBN 0-88839-276-1

Spirit Quest
Carol Batdorf
ISBN 0-88839-210-9

Tlingit
Dan & Nan Kaiper
ISBN 0-88839-010-6

Totem Poles of the NW
D. Allen
ISBN 0-919654-83-5

Western Indian Basketry
Joan Megan Jones
ISBN 0-88839-122-6

When Buffalo Ran
George Bird Grinnell
ISBN 0-88839-258-3

ESKIMO TITLES

Eskimo Life Yesterday
Hancock House
ISBN 0-919654-73-8

The Incredible Eskimo
de Coccola & King
ISBN 0-88839-189-7

Life with the Eskimo
Hancock House
ISBN 0-919654-72-X